The H

THAMES

The Historic

THAMES

A Portrait of England's Greatest River

HILAIRE BELLOC

I.B. TAURIS

LONDON · NEW YORK

Published in 2008 by I.B.Tauris & Co Ltd
6 Salem Road, London W2 4BU
175 Fifth Avenue, New York NY 10010
www.ibtauris.com

In the United States of America and Canada distributed by Palgrave Macmillan,
a division of St. Martin's Press, 175 Fifth Avenue, New York NY 10010

ISBN: 978 1 84511 712 2

A full CIP record for this book is available from the British Library
A full CIP record is available from the Library of Congress

Library of Congress Catalog Card Number: available

Typeset in Perpetua by A. & D. Worthington, Newmarket, Suffolk
Printed and bound in Great Britain by TJ International Ltd, Padstow, Cornwall

THE HISTORIC THAMES

England has been built up upon the framework of her rivers, and, in that pattern, the principal line has been the line of the Thames.

Partly because it was the main highway of Southern England, partly because it looked eastward towards the Continent from which the national life has been drawn, partly because it was better served by the tide than any other channel, but mainly because it was the chief among a great number of closely connected river basins, the Thames Valley has in the past supported the government and the wealth of England.

Among the most favoured of our rivals some one river system has developed a province or a series of provinces; the Rhine has done so, the Seine and the Garonne. But the great Continental river systems – at least the navigable ones – stand far apart from one another: in this small, and especially narrow, country of Britain navigable river systems are not only numerous, but packed close together. It is perhaps on this account that we have been under less necessity in the past to develop our canals; and anyone who has explored the English rivers in a light boat knows how short are the portages between one basin and another.

Now not only are we favoured with a multitude of

navigable waterways – the tide makes even our small coastal rivers navigable right inland – but also we are quite exceptionally favoured in them when we consider that the country is an island.

If an island, especially an island in a tidal sea, has a good river system, that system is bound to be of more benefit to it than would be a similar system to a Continental country. For it must mean that the tide will penetrate everywhere into the heart of the plains, carrying the burden of their wealth backward and forward, mixing their peoples, and filling the whole national life with its energy; and this will be especially the case in an island which is narrow in proportion to its length and in which the rivers are distributed transversely to its axis.

When we consider the river systems of the other great islands of Europe we find that none besides our own enjoys this advantage. Sicily and Crete, apart from the fact that they do not stand in tidal water, have no navigable rivers. Iceland, standing in a tidal sea, too far north indeed for successful commerce, but not too far north for the growth of a civilisation, is at a similar disadvantage. Great Britain and Ireland alone – Great Britain south of the Scottish Mountains, that is – enjoy this peculiar advantage; and there are few things more instructive when one is engaged upon the history of England than to take a map and mark upon it the head of each navigable piece of water and the head of its tideway, for when this has been done all England, with the exception of the Welsh Hills and the Pennines, seems to be penetrated by the influence of the sea.

The conditions which give a river this great historic

PEGASUS BOOKS, OAKLAND
5560 College Ave.
Oakland, Ca. 94618
(510) 652-6259

B   43761 11/28/2010 05:16 PM

00005	1 Used CDs	8.00	8.00
00008	1 Postage	9.00	9.00
10001	1 Used Book	7.50	7.50
10001	1 Used Book	3.00	3.00
30000	1 Stax	7.99	7.99
*NBS	Historic Tha	26.00	26.00

	Subtotal:	5	61.49
	Tax:		5.12
CLERK	Total Due:		66.61
	Bank Card		66.61

Thank You!

Merchandise may be exchanged for store
credit only, with receipt, for 7 days.

*****
***
*

importance, the fundamental character, therefore, which has lent to the Thames its meaning in English history, is twofold: a river affords a permanent means of travel, and a river also forms an obstacle and a boundary. Men are known to have agglomerated in the beginning of society in two ways: as nomadic hordes and as fixed inhabitants of settlements.

There has arisen a profitless discussion as to which of these two phases came first. No evidence can possibly exist upon either side, but one may take it that with the first traditions and records, as at the present time, the two systems existed side by side, and that either was determined by geographical conditions. A river is an advantage to both groups, but to the second it is of more consequence than to the first; and in South England, if we go back to the origins of our history, it is in fixed settlements that we find the first evidence of man. With every year of research the extreme antiquity of our inhabited sites becomes more apparent. And indeed the geographical nature of Southern England should make us certain of the antiquity of village life in it, even were there no archæological evidence to support that antiquity.

South England is everywhere fertile, everywhere well watered, and nowhere divided, as is the North, by long districts of bare country, or of hills snowbound in winter, or of morass. Its forests, though numerous, have never formed one continuous belt; even the largest of them, the Forest of the Weald, between the downs of Surrey and Kent and those of Sussex, was but twenty miles across – large enough to nourish a string of hunting villages upon the north and the south edges of it; but not large enough to isolate the Thames Valley from the southern coast.

From the beginning of human activity in this island the whole length of the river has been set with human settlements never far removed one from the other; for the Thames ran through the heart of South England, and wherever its banks were secure from recurrent floods it furnished those who settled on them with three main things which every early village requires: good water, defence, and communication.

The importance of the first lessens as men learn to dig wells and to canalise springs; the two last, defence and communication, remain attached to river settlements to a much later date, and are apparent in all the history of the Thames.

The problem of communication under early conditions is serious. Even in a high civilisation the maintenance of roads is of greater moment, and imposes a greater burden, than most of the citizens who support it know; but before the means or the knowledge exist to survey and to harden roads, with their causeways over marshes and their bridges over rivers, the supply of food in time of scarcity or of succour in time of danger is never secure: a little narrow path kept up by nothing but the continual passage of men and animals is all the channel a community of men have for communicating with their neighbours by land. And it must be remembered that upon such communication depend not only the present existence, but the future development of the society, which cannot proceed except by that fertilisation, as it were, which comes from the mixture of varied experiences and of varied traditions: every great change in history has necessarily been accompanied by some new activity of travel.

Under the primitive conditions of which we speak a river of moderate depth, not too rapid in its current and perennial in its supply, is much the best means by which men may communicate. It will easily carry, by the exertions of a couple of men, some hundred times the weight the same men could have carried as porters by land. It furnishes, if it is broad, a certain security from attack during the journey; it will permit the rapid passage of a large number abreast where the wood tracks and paths of the land compel a long procession; and it furnishes the first of the necessities of life continually as the journey proceeds.

Upon all these accounts a river, during the natural centuries which precede and follow the epochs of high civilisation, is as much more important than the road or the path as, let us say, a railway to-day is more important than a turnpike.

What is equally interesting, when a high civilisation after its little effort begins to decline into one of those long periods of repose into which all such periods of energy do at last decline, the river reassumes its importance. There is a very interesting example of this in the history of France. Before Roman civilisation reached the north of Gaul the Seine and its tributary streams were evidently the chief economic factors in the life of the people: this may be seen in the sites of their strongholds and in the relation of the tribes to one another, as for instance, the dependence of the Parisians upon Sens. The five centuries of active Roman civilisation saw the river replaced by the system of Roman roads; the great artificial track from north to south, for instance, takes on a peculiar importance; but when the end of that period has come, and the energies of the Roman state are beginning to drag, when the money cannot be collected to repair the great highways, and these fall into decay – then the Seine and its tributaries reassume their old importance. Paris, the junction of the various waterways, becomes the capital of a new state, and the influence of its kings leads out upon every side along the river valleys which fall into the main valley of the Seine.

There are but two considerable modifications to the use for habitation of slow and constant rivers: their value is lessened or interrupted by precipitous banks or they are rendered unapproachable by marshes. The first of these causes, for instance, has singularly cut off one from the other the groups of population residing upon the upper and the lower Meuse, as it has also, to quote another example, cut off even in language the upper from the lower Elbe.

From this first species of interruption the Thames is, of course, singularly free. There is no river in England, with the exception of the Trent, whose banks interfere so little with the settlement of men in any place on account of their steepness.

As to the second, the Thames presents a somewhat rare character.

The upper part of the river, which is in lowland valleys the most easily inhabited, and the part in which, once the river is navigable, will be found the largest number of small settlements, is in the case of the Thames the most marshy.

From its source to beyond Cricklade the river runs entirely over clay; thenceforward the valley is a flat mass of alluvium, in which the stream swings from one side to the other, and even where it touches higher soil, touches nothing better than the continuation of this clay. In spite, therefore, of the shallowness and narrowness of the upper river there always existed this impediment which an insecure soil would present to the formation of any considerable settlements. The loneliness of the stretch below Kelmscott is due to an original difficulty of this kind, and the one considerable settlement upon the upper river at Lechlade stands upon the only place where firm ground approaches the bank of the river.

This formation endures well below Oxford until one reaches the gap at Sandford, where the stream passes between two beds of gravel which very nearly approach either bank.

Above this point the Thames is everywhere, upon one side or the other, guarded by flat river meadows, which must in early times have been morass; and nowhere were these more difficult of passage than in the last network of streams between Witham Hill and Sandford, to the west of the gravel bank upon which Oxford is built.

Below Sandford, and on all the way to London Bridge, the character of the river in this respect changes. You have everywhere gravel or flinty chalk, with but a narrow bed of alluvial soil, upon either bank to represent the original overflow of the river.

At the crossing places (as we shall see later), notably at Long Wittenham, at Wallingford, at Streatley, at Pangbourne, and, still lower, at Maidenhead and at Ealing, this hard soil came right down to the bank upon either side.

On all this lower half of the Thames marsh was rare, and was to be found even in early times only in isolated patches, which are still clearly defined. These are never found facing each other upon opposite banks of the stream. Thus there was a bad bit on the left bank above Abingdon, but the large marsh below Abingdon, where the Ock came in, was on the right bank, with firm soil opposite it. There was a large bay, as it were, of drowned land on the right bank, from below Reading to a point opposite Shiplake, the last wide morass before the marshes of the tidal portion of the river; and another at the mouth of the Colne, above Staines, on the left bank, which was the last before one came to the mud of the tidal estuary; and even the tidal marshes were fairly firm above London. From Staines eastward down as far as Chelsea the superficial soil upon either side is of gravels, and the long list of ancient inhabited sites upon either bank show how little the overflow of the river interfered with its usefulness to men.

The river, then, from Sandford downward has afforded upon either bank innumerable sites upon which a settlement could be formed. Above Sandford these sites are not to be found indifferently upon either bank, but now on one, now on the other. There is no case on the upper river of two villages facing each other on either side of the stream. But though the soil of this upper part was in general less suited to the establishment of settlements, a certain number of firmer stretches could be found, and advantage was taken of them to build.

There thus arose along the whole course of the Thames from its source to London a series of villages and towns, increasing in importance as the stream deepened and gave greater facilities to traffic, and bound together by the common life of the river. It was their *highway*, and it is as a highway that it must first be regarded.

Of the way in which the Thames was a necessary great road in early times, perhaps the best proof is the manner in which various parishes manage to get their water front at the expense of a somewhat unnatural shape to their boundaries. Thus Fawley in Buckinghamshire has a curious and interesting arrangement of this sort thrusting down from the hills a tongue of land which ends in a sort of wharfage on the river just opposite Remenham church. In Berkshire there are also several examples of this. On the upper river Dractmoor and Kingston Bagpuise are both very narrow and long, a shape forced upon them by the necessity of having this outlet upon the river in days when the life of a parish was a real one and the village was a true and self-sufficing unit. Next to them Fyfield does the same thing. Lower down, near Wallingford, the parish of Brightwell has added on a similar eccentric edge to the north and east so that it may share in the bank; but perhaps the best example of all in this connection is the curious extension below Reading. Here land which is of no use for human habitation – water meadows continually liable to floods – runs out from the parish northward for a good mile. These lands are separated from the river during the whole of this extension until at last a bend of the stream gives the parish the opportunity it has evidently sought in thus extending its boundaries. On the Oxford bank Standlake and Bright-hampton do the same thing upon the Upper Thames and to some extent Eynsham; for when one thinks how far back Eynsham stands from the river it is somewhat remarkable that it should have claimed the right to get at the stream. Below Oxford there is another most interesting instance of the same thing in the case of Littlemore. Littlemore stands on high and dry land up above the river somewhat set back from it. Sandford evidently interfered with its access to the water, and Littlemore has therefore claimed an obviously artificial extension for all the world like a great foot added on to the bulk of the parish. This 'foot' includes Kenning-ton Island, and runs up the meadows to the foot of that eyot.

The long and narrow parishes in the reaches below Benson, Nuneham Morren, Mongewell, and Ipsden and South Stoke are not, however, examples of this tendency.

They owe their construction to the same causes as have produced the similar long parishes of the Surrey and the Sussex Weald. The life of the parish was in each case right on the river or very close to it, and the extension is not the attempt of the parish to reach the river, but the claim of the parish upon the hunting lands which lay up behind it upon the Chiltern Hills. The truth of this will be appar-ent to anyone who notes upon the map the way in which parishes are thus lengthened, not only on the western side of the hills, but also upon the farther eastern side, where there was no connection with the river.

There are many other proofs remaining of the chief function which the Thames fulfilled in the early part of our history as a means of communication.

We shall see later in these pages how united all that line of the stream has been; how the great monasteries founded upon the Thames were supported by possessions stretched all along the valleys; how much of it, and what important parts, were held by the Crown; and how strong was the architectural influence of towns upon one another up and down the water, as also how the place names upon the banks are everywhere drawn from the river; but before dealing with these it is best to establish the main portions into which the Thames falls and to see what would naturally be their limits.

It may be said, generally, that every river which is tidal, and whose stream is so slow as to be easily navigable in either direction, divides itself naturally, when one is regarding it as a means of communication, into three main divisions.

There will first of all be the tidal portion which the tide usually scours into an estuary. As a general rule, this portion is not considerably inhabited in the early periods of history, for it is not until a large international commerce arises that vessels have much occasion to stop as they pass up and down the maritime part of the stream; and even so, settlements upon its banks must come comparatively late in the development of the history of the river, because a landing upon such flooded banks is not easily to be effected.

This is true of the Dutch marshes at the mouths of the Rhine, whose civilisation (one exclusively due to the energy of man) came centuries after the establishment of the great Roman towns of the Rhine; it is true of the estuary of the

Seine, whose principal harbour of Havre is almost modern, and whose difficulties are still formidable for ocean-going craft; and it is true of the Thames.

The estuary of the Thames plays little or no part in the very early history of England. Invaders, when they landed, landed on the sea-coast at the very mouth, or appear to have sailed right up into the heart of the country.

It is, nevertheless, true that the last few miles of tidal water, in Western Europe at least, are not to be included in this first division of a great river.

The swish of the tide continues up beyond the broad estuary, the sand-banks, and the marshes, and there are reaches more or less long (rather less than twenty miles perhaps originally in the case of the Thames, rather more perhaps originally in the case of the lower Seine) which for the purposes of habitation are inland reaches. They have the advantage of a current moving in either direction twice a day and yet not the disadvantage of greatly varying levels of water. Thus one may say of the Seine in the old days that from about Caudebec to Point de L'Arche it enjoyed such inland tidal conditions; and of the Thames from Greenwich to Teddington that similar advantages existed.

The true point of division which separates, so far as human history is concerned, the lower from the upper part of such rivers is the first bridge, and, what almost always accompanies the first bridge, the first great town. To repeat the obvious parallel, Rouen was this point upon the Seine; upon the Thames this point was the Bridge of London. It is with the habitable and historic Thames Valley above the bridge that this book has to deal, and it will later be to the reader's purpose to consider why London Bridge crossed the stream just where it did, and of what moment that site has been in the history of the Thames and of England.

The second division in a great European tidal river, considered as a means of communication, is the navigable but non-tidal portion.

The word navigable is so vague that it requires some definition before we can apply it to any particular stream. It does not, of course, mean in this connection 'navigable by sea-going boats'. One may take a constant depth of so little as three feet to be sufficient for the purpose of carrying merchandise even in considerable bulk.

The legislatures of various countries have established varying gauges to determine where the navigability of a river may be said to cease. In practice these gauges have always been arbitrary. The upper reaches of a river may present sufficient depth but too fast a current, or they may be too narrow, or the curves may be too rapid, or the obstruction of rocks too common, for any sort of navigation, although the depth of water be sufficient.

Conversely, in some streams of peculiar breadth and constancy very shallow upper reaches may have early been converted to the use of man. The matter is only to be determined by the experience of what the inhabitants of a river valley have actually been able to do under the local circumstances, and when we examine this we shall usually be astonished to see how far inland a river was used until the history of internal navigation was transformed by the development of canals or partially destroyed by the development of railways. Thus it is certain that so small a stream as the Adur in Sussex floated barges up to the boundaries of Shipley Parish; that the Stour was habitually used beyond Canterbury; that so tiny a tributary as the Ant in Norfolk was followed up from its parent Bure to the neighbourhood of Worsted.

In this connection the Thames is of an especial interest, for it had, in proportion to its length, the greatest section of navigable non-tidal water of any of the shorter rivers in Europe. Until the digging of the Thames and Severn Canal at the end of last century it was possible, and even common, for boats to reach Cricklade, or at any rate the mouth of the Churn. And even now, in spite of the pumping that is necessary at Thames head and the consequent diminution of the volume of water in the upper reaches, the Thames, were water carriage to come again into general use, would be a busy commercial stream as high up as Lechlade.

This exceptional sector of non-tidal navigable water cutting right across England from east to west, and that in what used to be the most productive and is still the most fertile portion of the island, is the chief factor in the historic importance of the Thames.

From Cricklade to the navigable waters of the Severn Valley is but a long day's walk; and one may say that even in the earliest times there was thus provided a great highway right across what then was by far the most thickly populated and the most important part of the island.

A third section in all such rivers (and, from what we have said above, a short and insignificant one in the case of the Thames) may be called the *head-waters* of the river: where the stream is so shallow or so uncertain as to be no longer navigable. In the case of the Thames these headwaters cover no more than ten to fifteen miles of country. With the exception of rivers that run through mountain districts this section of a river's course is nearly always small in proportion to the rest; but the Thames, just as it has the longest proportion of navigable water, has also by far the shortest proportion of useless head-water of all the shorter European rivers.

There is a further discussion as to what is the true source of the Thames, and which streams may properly be regarded as its head-waters: the Churn, especially since the digging of the canal, having a larger flow than the stream from Thames head; but whichever is chosen, the non-navigable portion starts at the same point, and is the third of the divisions into which the valley ranges itself when it is considered in its length, as a highway from the west to the east of England. The two limits, then, are at London Bridge and at Cricklade, or rather at some point between Lechlade and Cricklade, and nearer to the latter.

But a river has a second topographical and historic function. It cannot only be considered longitudinally as a highway, it can also be considered in relation to transverse forces and regarded as an obstacle, a defence, and a boundary.

This function has, of course, been of the highest importance in the history of all great rivers, not perhaps so much so in the case of the Thames as in the case of swifter or deeper streams, but, still, more than has been the case with so considerable and so rapid a river as the Po in Lombardy or the uncertain but dangerous Loire in its passage through the centre of France. For the Thames Valley was that which divided the vague Mercian land from which we get our weights, our measures, and the worst of our national accent, and cut it off from that belt of the south country which was the head and the heart of England until the last industrial revolution of our history.

The Thames also has entered to a large, though hardly to a determining, extent into the military history of the country; to an extent which is greater in earlier than in later times, because with every new bridge the military obstacle afforded by the stream diminished. And finally, the Thames, regarded as an obstacle, was the cause that London Bridge concentrated upon itself so much of the life of the nation, and that the town which that bridge served, always the largest commercial city, became at last the capital of the island.

We have already said that the establishment of the site of London Bridge was a capital point in the history of the river and the principal line of division in its course. What were the topographical conditions which caused the river to be crossed at this point rather than at another?

It is always of the greatest moment to men to find some crossing for a great river as low down as may be towards the mouth. For the higher the bridge the longer the detour between, at the least, *two* provinces of the country which the river traverses. It is especially important to find such a crossing as low down as possible when the river is tidal and when it is flanked upon either side by great flooded marshes, as was and is the Thames. For under such conditions it is difficult, especially in primitive times, to cross habitually from one side to the other in boats.

Now it is a universal rule of early topography, and one which can be proved upon twenty of the old trackways of England, that the wild path which the earliest men used, when it approaches a river, seeks out a spur of higher and drier land, and if possible one directly facing another similar spur upon the far side of the water. It is a feature which the present writer continually observed in the exploration of the old British trackway between Winchester and Canterbury; it is similarly observable in the presumably British track between Chester and Manchester; and it is the feature which determined the site of London Bridge.

From the sea for sixty miles is a succession of what was once entirely, and is now still in great part, marshy land; or at least if there are no marshes upon one bank there will be marshes upon the other. In the rare places down stream where there is a fairly rapid rise upon either side of the river the stream is far too wide for bridging; and these marshes were to be found right up the valley until one struck the gravel at Chelsea: even here there were bad marshes on the farther shore.

There is in the whole or the upper stretch of the tidal water but one place where a bluff of high and dry land faces, not indeed land equally dry immediately upon the farther bank, but at least a spur of dry land which approaches fairly near to the main stream. If the modern contour lines be taken and laid out upon a map of London this spur will be found to project from Southwark northward directly towards the river, and immediately opposite it is the dry hill, surrounded upon three sides by river or by marsh, upon which grew up the settlement of London. Here, then, the first crossing of the Thames was certain to be made.

It is not known whether a permanent bridge existed before the Roman Conquest. It may be urged in favour of the negative argument that Cæsar had no knowledge of such a bridge, or at least did not march towards it, but crossed the river with difficulty in the higher reaches by a ford. And it may also be urged that a bridge across the Rhine was equally unknown in that time. But, the bridge once established, it could not fail to become the main point of convergence for the commerce of Southern England, and indeed for much of that which proceeded from the North upon its way to the Continent. Such an obstacle would oppose itself to every invasion, and did, in fact, oppose itself to more than one historical invasion from the North Sea. It would further prevent sea-going vessels whose masts were securely stepped and could not lower from proceeding farther up stream, and would thereupon become the boundary of the seaport of the Thames. Such a bridge would, again, concentrate upon itself the traffic of all that important and formerly wealthy part of the island which bulges out to the east between the estuary of the Thames and the Wash, and which must necessarily have desired communication both with the still wealthier southern portion and with the Continent. But, more important than this, London Bridge also concentrated upon itself all the up-country traffic in men and in goods which came in by the natural gate of the country at the Straits of Dover, except that small portion which happened to be proceeding to the south-west of England: and this exception to the early commerce of

England was the smaller from the comparative ease with which the Channel could be crossed between Brittany and Cornwall.

Finally, the Bridge, as it formed the limit for sea-going vessels, formed also if not the limit at least a convenient terminus for craft coming from inland down the stream. It would form the place of trans-shipment between the sea-going and the inland trade.

Everything then conspired to make this first crossing of the Thames the chief commercial point in Britain; and, since we are considering in particular the history of the river, it must be noted that these conditions also made of London Bridge what we have remarked it to be, the chief division in the whole course of the stream. This character it still maintains, and the life of the river from the bridge to the Nore is a totally different thing, with a different literature and a different accompanying art, from the life of the river above bridges.

We have seen that the river when it is regarded as an avenue of access to men for commerce or for travel is, especially in early times, and with boats of light draught, of one piece from Lechlade to London Bridge. There was in this section always sufficient water even in a dry summer to float some sort of a boat. But the river, regarded as a barrier or obstacle for human beings in their movement up and down Britain, did not form one such united section. On the contrary, it divided itself, as all such rivers do, into two very clearly defined parts: there was that upper part which could be crossed at frequent intervals by an army, that lower part in which fords are rare.

In most rivers one has nothing more to do in describing those two sections than to show how gradually they merge into one another. In most rivers the passage of the upper waters is perfectly easy, and as one descends the fords get rarer and rarer, until at last they cease.

With the Thames this is not the case. The two portions of the river are sharply divided in the vicinity of Oxford, and that for reasons which we have already seen when we were speaking of the suitability of its banks for habitation. The upper Thames is indeed shallow and narrow, and there are innumerable places above Oxford where it could be crossed, so far as the volume of its waters was concerned. It was crossed by husbandmen wherever a village or a farm stood upon its banks. Perhaps the highest point at which it had to be crossed at one chosen spot is to be discovered in the word Somer*ford* Keynes, but the ease with which the water itself could be traversed is apparent rather in the absence than in the presence of names of this sort upon the upper Thames. Shifford, for instance, which used to be spelt Siford, may just as well have been named from the crossing of the Great Brook as from the crossing of the Thames. The only other is Duxford.

While, however, the upper Thames was thus easy to cross where individuals only or small groups of cattle were concerned, the marshes on either side always made it difficult for an army. The records of early fighting are meagre, and often legendary, but such as they are you do not find the upper Thames crossed and recrossed as are the upper Severn or the upper Trent. There are two points of passage: Cricklade and Oxford, nor can the passage from Oxford be made westward over the marshes. It is confined to the ford going north and south.

Below Oxford, after the entry of the Cherwell, and from thence down to a point not very easily determined, but which is perhaps best fixed at Wallingford, the Thames is only passable at fixed crossings in ordinary weather, as at Sandford, where the hard gravels approach the bank upon either side, and at other places, each distant from the next by long stretches of river.

It is not easy, now that the river has been locked, to determine precisely where all these original crossings are to be found.

The records of Abingdon and its bridge make it certain that a difficult ford existed here; the name 'Burford' attached to the bridge points to the ancient ford at this spot. It is a name to be discovered in several other parts of England where there has been some ancient crossing of a river, as, for instance, the crossing of the Mole in Surrey by the Roman military road.

The next place below Abingdon may have been at Appleford, but was more likely between the high cliff at Clifton-Hampden and the high and dry spit of Long Witten-ham. Below this again for miles there was no easy crossing of the river.

The Thames was certainly impassable at Dorchester. The whole importance of Dorchester indeed in history lies in its being a strong fortified position, and it depends for its defence upon the depth of the river, which swirls round the peninsula occupied by the camp.

It has been conjectured that there was a Roman ford

or ferry at the east end of Little Wittenham Wood, where
it touches the river. The conjecture is ill supported. No
track leads to this spot from the south, and close by is an
undoubted ford where now stands Shillingford Bridge.

Below this again there was no crossing until one got
to Wallingford; and here we reach a point of the greatest
importance in the history of the Thames and of England.

Wallingford was not the lowest point at which the
Thames could ever be crossed. So far was this from being
the case that the *tidal* Thames could be crossed in several
places on the ebb, notably at the passage between Ealing
and Kew, where Kew Bridge now stands; and, as we shall
see, the Thames was passable at many other places. But the
special character of the passage at Wallingford lay in the
fact that it was a ford upon which one could always depend.
Below Wallingford the crossings were either only to be
effected in very dry seasons or, though normally usable,
might be interrupted by rain.

It is at Wallingford, therefore, that the main lowest
passage of the Thames was effected, and it was through
Wallingford that Berkshire communicated with the Chilterns. Wallingford is, then, the second point of division upon
the Thames when one is regarding that river as a defence or
a boundary. Below Wallingford there was perhaps a regular
crossing at Pangbourne; there was certainly a ford of great
importance between Streatley and Goring; and all the way
down the river at intervals were difficult but practicable
passages – notably at Cowey Stakes between the Surrey and
the Middlesex shore, a place which is the traditional crossing
of Cæsar. The water here in normal weather was, however,

as much as five feet deep, and this ford well illustrates the difficulties of all the lower crossings of the Thames.

The effect of the river as a barrier must, of course, have largely depended upon the level to which the waters rose in early times. It is exceedingly difficult to get any evidence upon this – first, because however far you go back in English history some sort of control seems always to have been imposed upon the river; and secondly, because the early overflows have left little permanent effect.

As an example of the antiquity of the regulation of the Thames we have the embankment round the Isle of Dogs, which is Roman or pre-Roman in its origin, like the sea-wall of the Wash, which defends the Fenland; and at Ealing, Staines, Abingdon, and twenty other places we have sites probably pre-historic, and certainly at the beginnings of history, which could never have been inhabited if the neighbouring fields had not been drained or protected. The regularity of the stream has therefore been somewhat artificial throughout all the centuries of recorded history, and the banks have had ample time to acquire consistency.

It is certain, of course, that works of planting, of draining, or of embankment, which required continuous energy, skill, and capital, decayed after the coming of the Saxon pirates, and were not undertaken again with full vigour until after the Norman Conquest. Even to-day the work is not quite complete, though every year sees its improvement: we are still unable to prevent regularly recurrent floods in the flats round Oxford and below the gorge of the Chilterns; but for the purpose of this argument the chief fact to be noted is that no serious interruption to the approach of the river seems to have existed in historic times.

In pre-historic times many stretches of the river must have afforded great difficulties of approach. The mouths of the Ock, the Coln, the Kennet, the Mole, and the Wandle must each have been surrounded by a marsh; all the plain between Oxford and the Hinkseys must have been partially flooded, as must the upper reaches between Lechlade and Witham (on one side or the other of the stream as it winds from the southern to the northern rises of land), and as must also have been the long stretch of the right bank below Reading. The highest spring tides may have been felt as high up the stream as Staines, and both the character of the surface and the contour lines permit one to conjecture that the valley of the Wandle and several other inlets from the lower river were flooded. Yet it is remarkable that in this alluvium, more disturbed and dug than any other in Europe, little or nothing of human relics, of boats, or of piles has been discovered, and this absence of testimony also points to the remoteness of date from which we should reckon the human control of the river.

Here, as in many other conjectures concerning early history or pre-history, one is convinced of that safe rule which, in Europe at least, bids us never exaggerate the changes achieved by the last few centuries or the contrast between recorded and unrecorded things.

The tendency of most modern history in this country has been to exaggerate such changes and such contrasts. In the greater part of modern popular history care is taken to emphasise the difference between the Middle and Dark Ages and the last few centuries. The forests of England are represented as impassable, or nearly so; the numbers of the population are grossly underestimated; the towns which have had a continuous municipal existence of 1500 years are represented as villages.

The same spirit would tend to make of the Thames Valley in the Dark and Middle Ages a very different landscape from that which we see to-day. The floods were indeed more common and the passage of the river somewhat more difficult; cultivation did not everywhere approach the banks as it does now; and in two or three spots where there has been a great development of modern building, notably at Reading, and, of course, in London, the banks have been artificially strengthened. But with these exceptions it may be confidently asserted that no belt of densely inhabited landscape in England has changed so little in its natural features as the Thames Valley.

There are dozens of reaches upon the upper Thames where little is in sight save the willows, the meadows, and a village church tower, which present exactly the same aspect to-day as they did when that church was first built. You might put a man of the fifteenth century on to the water below St John's Lock, and, until he came to Buscot Lock, he would hardly know that he had passed into a time other than his own. The same steeple of Lechlade would stand as a permanent landmark beyond the fields, and, a long way off, the same church of Eaton Hastings, which he had known, would show above the trees.

There is another method of judging the comparative smallness of the change, and it is a method which can be applied to many other parts of England whose desertion or wildness in the Dark and early Middle Ages has been too confidently asserted. That method is to note where human settlements were and are found. With the exception of the long and probably marshy piece between Radcot and Shifford the whole of the upper Thames was dotted with such settlements, which, though small, were quite close to the banks. Kelmscott is right up against the river in what one would otherwise have imagined to be land too marshy for building until modern times. Buscot, on the other bank, is not only close to the river, but was a royal manor of high historical importance in the eleventh century. Eaton Hastings is similarly placed right against the bank; so was in its day the palace of Kempsford above Lechlade, and so is the church of Inglesham between the two. All the way down you have at intervals old stonework and old place names, indicating habitation upon the upper Thames.

A proper system of locks is comparatively modern on any European river. The invention is even said (upon doubtful authority) to be as late as the sixteenth century, but the method of regulating the waters of a river by weirs is immemorial.

We have no earlier record of weirs upon the Thames than that in Magna Charta; but some such system must have existed from the time when men first used the Thames in a regular manner for commerce.

There is but one place left in which one can still reconstruct for oneself the aspect of such weirs as were till but little more than a century ago the universal method of canalising the river. Modern weirs are merely adjuncts to locks, and are usually found upon a branch of the stream

other than that which leads up to the lock. But in this
weir the old fashion of crossing the whole stream is still
preserved. There is no lock, and when a boat would pass
up or down the paddles of the weir have to be lifted. It is,
in a modern journey upon the upper Thames, the one faint
incident which the day affords, for if one is going down
the stream but few paddles are lifted, and the boat shoots
a small rapid, while to admit a boat going up stream the
whole weir is raised, and, even so, a great rush of water
opposes the boat as it is hauled through. Some years ago
there were several of these weirs upon the upper river.
They have all been superseded by locks, and it is probable
that this last one will not long survive.

Such weirs did certainly sufficiently regulate the stream
as to make its banks regularly habitable. If no local order,
at least the interest of villagers in their mills sufficed to the
watching of the stream.

We have in the place names upon the Thames a further
evidence of the antiquity of its regulation, for, as will be
seen in a moment, none give proof of any important settlement later than the eleventh century.

These place names not only indicate a continuous and
early settlement of the banks, but also form in themselves
a very interesting series, whose etymology is a little section
of the history of England.

Of purely Celtic names very few survive in the sites of
human habitation, though the names of the waterways are
almost universally Celtic, as is the name of Thames itself.
But it is probable that in the Saxon names which line the
river there are many corruptions of Celtic words made to

sound in the Saxon fashion. We cannot prove such origins. We can surmise with justice that the 'tons' and 'dons' all up and down England are Celtic terminations; they are almost unknown in Germany. There is a somewhat pedantic guess, drawn (it is said) from Iceland, that we got this national name ending from Scandinavia; so universal a habit would hardly have arisen from an admixture of Scandinavian blood received at the very close of the Dark Ages and affecting but small patches of North England. Moreover, as against this theory, there is the fact that quite half the Celtic place names mentioned in our early history and in that of Gaul had a similar termination. London itself is the best example.

If, however, we neglect this termination, and consider the first part of the words in which it occurs (as in Abingdon, Bensing-ton, Ea-ton, etc.), we shall find that most of the place names are Saxon in form, and some certainly Saxon in derivation.

Thus Ea-ton, a name scattered all along the Thames, from its very source to the last reaches, is the 'tun' by the water or stream. Clif-ton (as in Clifton-Hampden) is the 'ton' on the cliff, a very marked feature of the left bank of the river at this place. Of Bensing-ton, now Benson, we know nothing, nor do we of the origin of the word Abingdon.

The names terminating in 'ham' are, in their termination at least, certainly Teutonic; and the same may be true of most of those – but not all of those – ending in 'ford'. Ford may just as well be a Celtic as a Teutonic ending, and in either case means a 'passage', a 'going'. It does not even in all cases indicate a shallow passage, though in the great majority of cases on the Thames it does indicate a place where one could cross the river on foot. Thus Wallingford was probably the walled or embattled ford, and Oxford almost certainly the 'ford of the droves' – droves going north from Berkshire. One may say roughly that all the 'hams' were Teutonic save where one can put one's finger on a probable Celtic derivation such as one has, for instance, in the case of Witham, which should mean the settlement upon the 'bend' or curve of the river, a Celtic name with a Teutonic ending.

One may also believe that the termination 'or' or 'ore' is Teutonic; Cumnor may have meant 'the wayfarers' stage', and Windsor probably 'the landing place on the winding of the river'.

Hythe also is thought to be Teutonic. One can never be quite sure with a purely Anglo-Saxon word, that it had a German origin, but at least Hythe is Anglo-Saxon, a wharf or stage; thus Bablock Hythe on the road through the Roman town of Eynsham across the river to Cumnor and Abingdon, cutting off the great bend of the river at Witham; so also the town we now call 'Maidenhead', which was perhaps the 'mid-Hythe' between Windsor and Reading. Some few certainly Celtic names do survive: in the Sinodun Hills, for instance, above Dorchester; and the first part of the name Dorchester itself is Celtic. At the very head of the Thames you have Coates, reminding one of the Celtic name for the great wood that lay along the hill; but just below, where the water begins to flow, Kemble and Ewen, if they are Saxon, are perhaps drawn from the presence of a 'spring'.

Cricklade may be all Celtic, or may be partly Celtic and partly Saxon. London is Celtic, as we have seen. And in the mass of places whose derivation it is impossible to establish the primitive roots of a Celtic place name may very possibly survive.

The purely Roman names have quite disappeared, and, what is odd, they disappeared more thoroughly in the Thames Valley than in any other part of England. Dorchester alone preserves a faint reminiscence of its Romano-Celtic name; but Bicester to the north, and the crossing of the ways at Alchester, are probably Saxon in the first part at least. Streatley has a Roman derivation, as have so many similar names throughout England which stand upon a 'strata' or 'way' of British or of Roman origin. But though 'Spina' is still Speen, Ad Pontes, close by, one of the most important points upon the Roman Thames, has lost its Roman name entirely, and is known as Staines: the stones or stone which marked the head of the jurisdiction of London upon the river.

To return to the river regarded as a *boundary*, it is subject to this rather interesting historical observation that it has been more of a boundary in highly civilised than in barbaric times.

One would expect the exact contrary to be the case. A civilised man can cross a river more easily than a barbarian; and in civilised times there are permanent bridges, where in barbaric times there would be only fords or ferries.

Nevertheless, it is true of the Thames, as of nearly every other division in Europe, that it was much more of a boundary at the end of the Roman Empire, and is more of a strict boundary to-day, than it was during the Dark Ages, and presumably also before the Claudian invasion. Thus we may conjecture with a fair accuracy that in the last great ordering of boundaries within the Roman Empire, which was the work of Diocletian, and so much of which still survives in our European politics to-day (for instance, the boundary of Normandy), the Thames formed the division between Southern and Midland Britain. It is equally certain that it did *not* form any exact division between Wessex and Mercia.

The estuary has, of course, always formed a division, and in the barbarian period it separated the higher civilisation of Kent from that of the East Saxons, who were possibly of a different race, and certainly of a different culture. But the Thames above London Bridge was not a true boundary until the civilisation of England began to form, towards the close of the Dark Ages. It is perpetually crossed and recrossed by contending armies, and the first result of a success is to cause the conqueror to annex a belt from the farther bank to his own territories.

It is further remarkable that the one great definite boundary of the Dark Ages in England – that which was established for a few years by Alfred between his kingdom and the territory of the Danish invaders – abandons the Thames above bridges altogether, and uses it as a limitation in its estuarial part only, up to the mouth of the Lea.

With the definition of exact frontiers for the English counties, however, a process whose origin can hardly antedate the Norman Conquest by many years, the Thames at once becomes of the utmost importance as a boundary.

Its higher and hardly navigable streams are not so used. The upper Thames and its little tributaries for some ten miles from its source are not only indifferent to county boundaries, but run through a territory which has been singularly indefinite in the past. For instance, the parish of Kemble, wherein the first waters now appear, has been counted now in Gloucester, now in Wilts. But when these ten miles are run, just after Castle Eaton Bridge, and not quite half way between that bridge and the old royal palace at Kempsford, the Thames becomes the line of division between two counties, and from there to the sea it never loses its character of a boundary.

It is a tribute to the great place of the river in history that there is no other watercourse in England nor any other natural division of which this is so universally true.

The reason that the Thames, like so many other European boundaries, has come late into the process of demarcation, and the reason that its use as a limit is more apparent in civilised than in uncivilised times, is simply the fact that limits and boundaries themselves are never of great exactitude save in times of comparatively high civilisation. It is when a complex system of law and a far-reaching power of execution are present in a country that the necessity for precise delimitation arises. In the barbaric period of England there was no such necessity. Doubtless the men of Berkshire and the men of Oxfordshire felt themselves to be in general divided by the stream; but had we documents to hand (which, of course, we have not) it might be possible to show that exceptional tracts, such as the isolated Hill of Witham (which is much more influenced by Oxford than by Abingdon), was treated as the land of Oxfordshire men in early times, or was perhaps a territory in dispute; and something of the same sort may have existed in the connection of Caversham with Reading.

In this old age of our civilisation the exactitude of the boundary which the Thames establishes is apparent in various survivals. Islands now joined to the one bank and indistinguishable from the rest of the shore are still annexed to the farther shore. Such a patch is to be found at Streatley, geographically in Berkshire, legally in Oxford; there is another opposite Staines, which Middlesex claims from Surrey.

In all, half-a-dozen or more such anomalous frontiers mark the course of the old river. One arrested in process of formation may be seen at Pentonhook.

A boundary – that is, an obstacle to travel – has this further feature, that the point at which it is crossed – that is, the point at which the obstacle is surmounted – is certain to become a point of strategic and often of commercial importance. So it is with the passes over mountains and with the narrows of the sea, and so it is with fords and bridges over rivers. So it is with the Thames.

The energies both of travel and of war are driven towards and confined in such spots. Fortresses arise and towns which they may defend. Depots of goods are formed, the coining and the change of money are established, secure meeting places for speculation are founded.

Such passages over the Thames were of two sorts: there are first the original fords, numerous and primeval; next the crossing places of the great roads.

Of the original fords we have already drawn up a list. Few have, merely as fords, proved to be of strategic or commercial value. Oxford may have been an early exception; and the difficult passage at Abingdon founded a great monastery but no military post: the rise of each was connected, as was Reading (which had no ford), with the junction of a tributary. Wallingford alone, in its character of the last easy and practicable ford down the river, had for centuries an importance certainly due to geographical causes alone. Two principal events of English history – the crossing of the Thames by the Conqueror and the successful challenge of Henry II to Stephen – depend upon the site of this crossing. Long before their time it had been of capital importance to the Saxon kings, so early as Offa and so late as Alfred. If the bridges built at Abingdon in the fifteenth century had not gradually deflected the western road, Wallingford might still count the fourteen churches and the large population which it possessed for so many centuries.

Apart from Wallingford, however, the fords, as fords, did little to build up towns or to determine the topography of English history. Of more importance were the crossings of the great *roads*.

When one remembers that the south of England was originally by far the wealthiest part of the country, and when one considers the shape of Ireland, it is evident that certain main tracks would lead from north to south, and that most or all of these would be compelled to cross the Thames Valley. We find four such primeval ways.

One from the Straits of Dover in the south-east to the north-western centres of the Welsh Marches and of Chester, the Port for Ireland, and so up west of the Pennines. This came in Saxon times to be called the *Watling Street*, a name common to other lesser lanes.

Another, the converse to this, proceeded from the metal mines of the south-west to the north-east until it struck and merged into other roads running north and east of the Pennines. This came to be called (as did other lesser roads) the *Fosse Way*.

A third went more sharply west from the southern districts, and connected them not with the Dee, but with the lower Severn. This track ran from the open highlands of Hampshire through Newbury and the Berkshire Hills to Gloucester, and was called (like other lesser tracks) the *Ermine Street*.

Finally, a fourth went in a great bend from these same highlands up eastward to the coast of the North Sea in East Anglia. This was called in Saxon times the *Icknield Way*.

All these can be traced in their general direction throughout and for most of their length minutely. All were forced to cross the Thames Valley, which so nearly divided the whole of South England from east to west.

Of these four crossings the first in point of interest is that which the *Ermine Street* makes over the upper Thames at *Cricklade*.

These old roads are of capital importance in the story of England, and though historians have always recognised this there are a number of features about them which have not been sufficiently noted – as, for instance, that armies until perhaps the twelfth century perpetually used them; for the great English roads, though their general track was laid out in pre-historic times, were generally hardened, straightened, and embanked by the Romans in a manner which permitted them to survive right on into the early Middle Ages; and of these four all were so hardened and strengthened, except the Icknield Way. Not one of them is quite complete to-day, but the Ermine Street is perhaps the best preserved. It is a good modern road all the way from Bayden to Gloucester, with the exception of a very slight gap at this village of Cricklade.

It originally crossed the river half-a-mile below Cricklade Bridge, so that the priory which stood on the left bank lay just to the south of the old road. How and when the old bridge at Cricklade fell we have no record, but one of the most important records of the Thames in Anglo-Saxon history is connected with this passage of the river.

The importance of Cricklade as a station upon the upper Thames does not only proceed from its being the crossing place of a great road, it is also the point when the first important tributary stream, the Churn, joins the Thames. Above this junction the Thames nowadays is hardly a stream; and even in the eighteenth century and earlier, before the digging of the Thames and Severn Canal, it must have depended on the weather whether there were any appreciable amount of water in the upper part or not. It would probably be found, if records could be examined, that the mills at Somerford Keynes were not continually worked throughout the year, even when the supply of water had been left undiminished by modern engineering. But when once the Churn (which, as we have seen, has a larger volume of water than the Thames) had fallen in at Cricklade

the two formed a true river, with depth in it always sufficient to support a boat, and with a fairly strong stream, as
also with a width sufficient for minor traffic; and it is after
Cricklade that you get a succession of villages and churches
dependent upon the river and standing close to its banks.

But though this piece of hydrography has its importance
the chief meaning of Cricklade in history lay in the fact
that it was the spot where this Ermine Street on its way
from the south country to the Severn Valley got over the
Thames, and the village connected with it was entrenched
certainly in Roman and probably in pre-Roman times. This
entrenchment may still be traced.

The crossing of the Thames by the Icknield Way, unlike
the crossing of the Ermine Street at Cricklade, presents a
problem.

Cricklade, as we have seen, is a perfectly well-established
site, and we owe our certitude upon the matter to the fact
that the Romans had hardened and straightened what was
probably an old British track. But with the crossing of the
Icknield Way no such complete certitude exists, for the
Icknield Way was but a vague barbarian track, often tortu-
ous in outline, confused by branching ways, and presenting
all the features of a savage trail. Doubtless that trail was
used during the four hundred years of the high Roman civilisation as a country road, just as the similar trail, known as
the 'Pilgrims' Way' from Winchester to Canterbury, was
used in the same epoch. There are plenty of Roman remains
to be found along the track, and there is no doubt that all
such roads, even when the State was not at the expense
of hardening or straightening them, were in continual use

before, as they were in continual use after, the presence of Roman government in this island; but the Icknield Way does not approach the river in a clear and unmistakable manner as would a Roman or a Romanised road. It is on this account that the exact point of its crossing has been debated.

The problem is roughly this: the high and treeless chalk downs have been used from the beginning of human habitation in these islands as the principal highways, and any single traveller or tribe that desired in early times to get from the Hampshire highlands to the east and north of England must have begun by following the ridge of the Berkshire Hills, and by continuing along the dry upland of the Chiltern Hills, which continue this reach beyond the Thames. But the spot at which the pre-historic crossing of the Thames was effected cannot be determined by a simple survey of the place where the Thames cuts through the chalk range. Wallingford up above this gorge has certain claims, both because it was the lowest of the continually practicable fords upon the river, and because its whole history points to an immemorial antiquity. Higher still, Dorchester, on which every historian of the Thames must dwell as perhaps the most interesting of all the settlements upon the banks of the river, has also been suggested. Just above Dorchester, on the Berkshire side, stands the peculiar isolated twin height which forms so conspicuous a landmark when one gazes over the plain from the summit of the Downs. Such landmarks often helped to trace the old roads. And Dorchester has also an immemorial antiquity – a pre-historic fortification upon the hills above, and fortifications, probably historic, on the Oxford bank below, but Dorchester has no ford.

When all the evidence is weighed it seems more probable that the regular crossing from the Berkshire Hills to the Chilterns was effected at Streatley.

Of this there are several proofs. In the first place, the name of the place suggests the passage of some great way. Place names of this sort are invariably found upon some one of the principal roads of England. In the second place, a lane bearing the traditional name of the Icknield Way can be traced to a point very near the river and the village. Another can be recovered beyond the river. The name would hardly have been so continued – even with considerable gaps – both upon the Oxfordshire and the Berkshire side unless the place of regular crossing had been here.

Within a mile or two of Streatley this lane begins to descend the side of the Berkshire Downs. Just before it falls into the Wantage Road and is lost it has begun to curl round the shoulder of the steep hill; but there is no way of telling at what precise spot it would strike the river upon the Berkshire side, because a thousand years or so of building, cultivation, and other changes have obliterated every trace of it.

Luckily, we have some indication upon the farther bank. A way can then be traced here as a lane (and in the gaps as a right of way, as a path, or sometimes only by its general direction) for some miles on the Oxfordshire side as it approaches Goring and the river coming from the Chilterns. And we know the point at which it strikes the village. This point is at the Sloane Hotel close to the railway; the inn is actually built upon the old road. Beyond the railway the track is continued in the lane which leads on past the schoolhouse to the old ferry, where there was presumably in Roman times a ford. If we accept this track we can conjecture that the vicarage of Streatley, upon the Berkshire bank, stands upon the continuation of the Way, and give the place where the pre-historic road crossed the river with tolerable certitude, though it is, I believe, impossible to recover the half-mile or so which lies between Streatley vicarage and the point where the Wantage Road and the Icknield Way separated upon the hillside above.

If the ford lay here the site was certainly well chosen, just below a group of islands which broadened the stream and made it at once shallower and less swift, acting somewhat as a natural weir above the crossing.

The third crossing place of a great pre-historic road, that of the Watling Street, is believed to correspond with the line of that very ugly suspension bridge which runs from Lambeth to the Horseferry Road in Westminster. This is, according to the most probable conjecture, the place at which the great road which ran from the Straits of Dover to the north-western ports of the island crossed the Thames.

Here, of course, there could be no question of a ford; there can only have been a ferry. Such a ferry existed throughout the Middle Ages and up to the building of Westminster Bridge, and produced a large revenue for the Archbishop of Canterbury. The memory of it is preserved in the name of the street upon the Middlesex shore. The Watling Street is fairly fixed in all its journey from the coast to the Archbishop's palace on the banks of the river.

On the Middlesex shore it is lost, but it may be conjectured to have run in a curve somewhere in the neighbourhood of Buckingham Palace up on the higher ground west of the Tybourne, parallel with or perhaps identical with Park Lane until we find it certainly again at the Marble Arch, whence in the form of the Edgware Road it begins a clear track across North-Western England.

As for the Fosse Way, it only just touches the valley of the Thames. It crosses the line of the river in a high embankment a mile or so below its traditional source at Thames head, but above the point where the first water is seen. A small culvert running under that embankment takes the flood water in winter down the hollow, but no longer covers a regular stream.

Besides these four crossings of the old British ways above London Bridge there is the crossing of the Roman Road at Staines, which may or may not represent a passage older than the Roman occupation. We have no proof of its being older. The river is deep, and, unless the broken causeway on the Surrey shore is regarded as the remains of British work, there is no trace of a pre-Roman track in the neighbourhood.

The crossing at Staines was the main bridge over the middle river during the Roman occupation; no other spot on the banks (except London Bridge) is *certainly* the site of a Roman bridge.

But apart from these there are two unsolved problems in connection with the roads across the Thames Valley in Roman times. The first concerns the passage of the upper Thames south of Eynsham; the second concerns the road which runs south from Bicester and Alchester.

As to the first of these, we know that the plain lying to the north of the Thames between the Cotswolds and the Chilterns was thoroughly occupied. We have also in the Saxon Chronicle a legendary account of the occupation of four Roman towns in this plain by the Saxon invaders. By what avenue did this wealthy and civilised district communicate with the wealthy and civilised south?

It is a question which will probably never be answered. There is no trace remaining of Roman bridges; perhaps nothing was built save of wood.

The obvious short-cut from the Roman town of Eynsham across the Witham peninsula to Abingdon bears no signs of a ford approached by Roman work or of a bridge, nor any record of such things.

As to the second question, the road from Bicester southward runs straight to Dorchester. At Dorchester, as we have seen, there was no ford, though just below it a Roman ferry has been guessed at.

There may have been a country road running down along the left or north bank of the river to the pre-historic crossing place at Goring and Streatley; but if there was, no trace of it remains, save perhaps in the two place names North Stoke and South Stoke.

A barrier has yet another quality in history, and that quality is perhaps the most important of all. In so far as it is an obstacle it is also a means of defence.

All the great rivers of Europe prove this. They are studded with lines of strongholds standing either right upon their banks or close by; and various as is the character of the different great rivers in their physical conformation, few or none have been unable to furnish sites for fortification. For instance, the slow rivers of Northern France, running for the most part through a flat country, were able to afford fortresses for the Gaulish clans in their numerous islands; the origin of Melun and Paris, for instance, was of this kind. The sharp rocks along the Rhône became platforms for castle after castle: Beaucaire, Tarascon, Aries, Avignon, and twenty others all of this sort.

The Thames, curiously enough, forms an exception; it is an exception even in the list of English rivers, most of which can show a certain number of fortifications along their banks.

In the whole course of the great river above London there are but three examples of fortification, or at any rate of fortification directly dependent upon the river. Of these the first, at Lechlade, is conjectural; the second, at Windsor, came quite late in history, and the only one which seems to have been a primeval fortified site was Dorchester.

There were, of course, plenty of towns and castles susceptible of defence. At one time or another every important settlement upon the Thames was capable of resistance: Oxford was walled, Wallingford was a fortress, Abingdon or Reading could be defended. But these were all, so to speak, artificial. The settlement came first, and after the settlement the necessity of guarding it from attack, and it was so guarded, not by natural means, but by human construction. The castle at Oxford, for instance, stood upon a mound of earth raised by human work. The only considerable place in which the river itself suggested defence from the earliest times appears to have been at Dorchester.

The curious importance of Dorchester in the very origins of English history and the still more curious way in which it sinks out of sight for generations, to revive again in the tenth century, is one of the puzzles of the history of the Thames.

It is useless to pursue an archæological discussion as to the origin of the place, and still more useless to try and determine why, though certainly the most easily defended, it should originally have been the *only* heavily fortified spot in the whole of the valley. We know that it was Roman: we know that it was a place of pre-historic fortification before the Romans came: we know that a Roman road ran northward towards Bicester from it, and we also know, or at least we can make a very probable guess, that though it was continuously important, and that the interest of early history is continually returning to it, it can never have been large.

Perhaps the best conjecture upon the origin of Dorchester is that the stronghold grew up as an out-lier to the great fort over the river at the top of Sinodun Hill. The exact and regular peninsula between the bend in the Thames and the mouth of the Thames is obviously suited for fortification: the tributary flows just to the east of this peninsula, exactly parallel with the main river beyond, and covers the peninsula not only with a stream on its east flank, but with a marsh at the mouth. One can imagine that the conspicuous heights of the Sinodun Hills were held, from the very beginning of human habitation in this district, as a permanent fortress, into which the neighbouring tribes could retire during war, and one can imagine that when the river was low in summer, and perhaps fordable, the spit of land before it, which formed an exception to the marshes round about, needed to be protected as a sort of bastion beyond the stream. This theory will at least account for the two great ridges of earthwork going from one water to the other and completely cutting off the peninsula, since it is agreed these works are earlier than the Roman invasion. Whatever its origin, the part which Dorchester plays in the early history of England is most remarkable.

The conversion of England was effected by a process of which we know far more than of any other series of national events before the Danish invasions. That process is more exactly recorded, less legendary, and more consecutively told because it was (to all contemporary watchers) the capital event of the time, and to all posterity the one thing that explained men to themselves.

We know also that, not so much the nucleus of the conversion as the secure vantage from which it marched outward, was the triangle of Kent. We can believe that the civilisation of Kent was something quite separate from the rest of the south-eastern portion of England, and that the many customary survivals which are, to this day, native to the county are remaining proofs of its unique character among the petty kingdoms during the mythical period between the withdrawal of the Romans and the arrival of St Augustine.

The early hold of civilisation upon Kent is explicable. But when the influence of Rome begins to spread again over

England you have distances covered which are astounding; there occur sporadic incidents of the highest importance in spots where they would be the least expected. Among the very first of these is the first baptism of a West-Saxon King.

It was certainly at Dorchester that this baptism took place and the choice of the site, little as we know of the village or city, has filled every historian with conjecture. Up to the very landing of St Augustine we are still dependent upon what is half legendary and very meagre record. The chief point indeed as regards this part of the country is the tradition of a battle fought against the British at Bedford by the West Saxons and the occupation of 'four towns'. This success was put down by tradition to the year 571, but everything was still so dark that even this success is a legend.

Within the lifetime of a man you have the baptism of Cynegil, the king of the West Saxons, at Dorchester, and that baptism takes place less than forty years after the complete submission of Kent.

The Chronicle, in mentioning this date, is no longer upon legendary ground: it is dealing with an event which was kept on record by civilised men who understood the art of writing, who could speak Latin, who could bear their records to Rome, and, what is more, the fact and the date are confirmed by the Venerable Bede.

It is imagined by some authorities that the fullness of the story and its apparent accuracy depend upon access to some early ecclesiastical record preserved at Dorchester and now lost. At any rate, Dorchester, whether because it had been, up till then, an unconquered Roman town, or for whatever other reason, becomes at once the ecclesiastical centre and one to which, even when this baptism takes place, the King of Northumbria was at the pains of travelling southward to, to be present as sponsor for the new Christian.

The story has a special historical interest, because it shows how very vague were the boundaries and the occupancies of the little wandering chieftains of this period. It need hardly be pointed out that no regular division into shires can have existed so early, and, as we have already insisted, the Thames itself was not a permanent boundary between any two definable societies, yet those who regard the Anglo-Saxon Chronicle as historical would show one Penda had appeared a few years before as the chief of a group of men with a new name, the Mercians – probably a loose agglomeration of tribes occupying the middle strip of England; a group whose dialect and measures of land are, perhaps, the ancestors of the modern Midland dialect and most of our measures. Cynegil's baptism could not have taken place in territory controlled by Penda, for he was the champion of all the Anti-Christian forces of the time, and though he had just defeated the West Saxons, and (according to a later legend) pushed back their boundary to the line of the Thames, his action, like that of all the little kings of the barbaric age in Britain, can have been no more than a march with a few thousands, a battle, and a retreat. In a word, the true and verifiable story of Cynegil's baptism is one of the many valuable instances which help to prove the unreliability of that part of the early Chronicle which does not deal with ecclesiastical affairs.

The priest who received Cynegil into the Church was one Birinus, an Italian, and perhaps a Milanese; he appears, from his first presence in Dorchester, to have fixed the seat of a bishopric in that village. His reasons for choosing the spot are as impossible to discover as are the origins of any other of the characteristics of the place. It was, in any case, as were so many of the sees of the Dark Ages, a frontier see – a sort of ecclesiastical fortress, pushed out to the very limits of the occupation of the enemy.

Whether Dorchester continued to be a bishopric from this moment onwards we cannot tell; but no less than three hundred years afterwards – in the tenth century – it appears again, and this time as the centre of the gigantic diocese which stretched throughout the whole of Middle England and right up to the Humber. The Conquest came, the diocese was cut up just afterwards, and the seat of the bishop finally removed from the village to Lincoln, and with the Conquest the importance of Dorchester as a fortified position, an importance which it had held for untold centuries, began to decline in favour of Oxford.

The artificial chain of fortifications up the Thames Valley, which had their origin under William the Conqueror, will call our attention to many other spots besides Oxford as these pages proceed, but it is interesting at this moment to consider Oxford in its early military aspect, when it succeeded Dorchester, and came forward as the chief stronghold of the upper Thames Valley above Wallingford.

The gravel bank north of the ford, by which what is presumed to have been the drovers' road from south to north crossed the river, had supported a very considerable

population, and had attained a very considerable civil importance, long before the Conquest. It is difficult to believe that
any new, especially that any extensive, centres of population
grew up in Anglo-Saxon Britain, upon sites chosen by the
barbarians. The Romans had colonised and densely populated every suitable spot. The ships' crews of open pirate
vessels had no qualities suitable to the founding of a town;
and when there is no direct evidence it is always safer of the
two conjectures in English topography to believe that any
spot which we find inhabited and flourishing in the Anglo-
Saxon period, even at its close, was not a town developed
during the Dark Ages but one which the pirates, when they
first entered the island, had found already inhabited and
flourishing, though sometimes perhaps more British than
Roman. But though this is always the more historical way
of looking at the probable origin of an English town it must
be admitted that there is no direct evidence of any town
upon the site of Oxford before the Danish invasions, and
the first mention of the place by name is as late as eleven
years after Alfred's death, when it is recorded that Edward,
his son, 'took possession of London and of Oxford and of
all lands in obedience thereunto'.

This first mention, slight as it is, characterises Oxford
as being the town of the upper Thames Valley at the opening of the tenth century, and we have what is usually a
good basis for history – that is, ecclesiastical tradition and a
monastic charter – to show us that a considerable monastery
had existed upon the spot for a century and a half before
this first mention in the Chronicle.

There still exists in the modern town, to the west of

it, a large artificial mound, one of those which have been discovered here and there up and down England, and which are characteristic of a late Saxon method of fortification. Before the advent of the Normans these mounds were defended by palisades only, and were used as but occasional strongholds. It may be conjectured that this Saxon work at Oxford dates from somewhat the same period as does the first mention of the town in the Chronicle. Twelve years later Alfred's grandson is mentioned as dying at Oxford. It may be presumed that his death would indicate the presence of a royal palace. We hear nothing more of this town during the remainder of the tenth century, but we have a long account in what is probably an accurate record of the rising of the townsmen against the Danes in the beginning of the eleventh. The Scandinavians made their last stand in the church of the monastery, and the townsmen burnt it. Five years later a new host of Danes took and burnt the town; and four years later again, Sweyn, in his terrible conquering march, captured it, after very little resistance, in the same year in which he took the crown of England. The brief episode of Edmund Ironside again brings the town into history: he slept here upon his way to London in the late autumn of 1016, and here, very probably, he was killed. From that moment the fortress (as it now certainly was) enters continually into that last anarchy which was only cured by a second advent of European civilisation and the success of its armies at Hastings.

The great national council of 1018, which may be called the settlement of Canute, was held at Oxford, and in 1036 another national council, of even greater importance, which was held to decide upon the succession of Canute's heirs, was again held at Oxford, and it was at Oxford that, four years later, the first Harold died.

Meanwhile, in the near neighbourhood of the city, at Islip, Queen Emma had, half a lifetime earlier, borne a son, who, after the death of all these Danes, remained the legitimate heir to the English throne. Islip was, most probably, not royal, but a private manor of the Queen's, which descended to the Confessor, and it is interesting to note in passing that it was his gift of this land and of its church to Westminster Abbey which originated the present connection between the two – a connection which has now, therefore, behind it nearly nine hundred years of continuity.

In the few hurried months before Hastings the last of the great Anglo-Saxon meetings in the town was summoned. It was held at the end of October 1065, and was that in which Harold's policy was agreed to. Within twelve months Harold himself was dead, and a victorious invading army was marching upon Wallingford.

In all this record it is clear that Oxford held a continually growing place in the life of England, and especially as a stronghold of whoever might be governing England. What battle was fought there, if any, or how the Normans got it, we do not know, but it is presumed that it suffered in the fighting because the number and value of its houses is given in the subsequent Survey as having fallen very largely indeed.

It is always well, whenever one comes across the Domesday Survey in history, to remember that the whole record is very imperfectly understood. We do not know quite what was being measured: we do not know, for instance, in the case of a town like Oxford, whether all the inhabited houses were counted; or whether only those who by custom gave taxes were counted; nor can we be certain of the meaning of the word *vastus*, save that it has some connection either with destruction or dilapidation, or lack of occupation, or, possibly, even remission of taxation. But the theory of a sack is not without foundation, for we know that in the case of York (which was certainly sacked by Tostig in 1065 and then again by William in 1068) what is probably a destruction of a similar kind, though a rather greater one, is expressed in similar words.

Whether, however, the number given in the town list of the Conqueror is or is not due to the destruction wrought by the Conquest we must be very careful not to estimate the population of that time upon the basis to-day such a list would afford. The figures of Domesday stand for a much larger population than most historians have hitherto been inclined to grant, as may be shown by considerations to which I shall only allude here, as I shall have to repeat them more fully upon a later page when I speak of urban life upon the Thames. The nomadic element in the life of the early Middle Ages; the smallness of the space allotted for sleeping; the large amount of time spent out of doors; the great proportion of collegiate institutions, not only monastic but military; the life in common which spread as a habit to so many parts of society beyond the monastic; the large families which (from genealogy) we can trust to be as much a character of the early Middle Ages as they, were not the character of the later Middle Ages, the crowd of semi-servile dependants which would be discovered in any large house – all these make us perfectly safe in multiplying by at least ten the number of households counted in the Survey if we would get at the population of those households, and it must be remembered that the houses counted, even in those parts of England which were fairly thoroughly surveyed, can only represent a *minimum* number, whatever was the method of counting. The lists may in some instances include every single household in a place, though from what we know of the diversity of local custom this is unlikely. In most places it is far more likely that the list covered but some portion that by custom owed a public tax, and this is especially true of the towns.

After Dorchester, which was the first of the fortresses of the Thames, so far as we have any knowledge, and after Oxford, which came next, and appears to have been founded since the beginning of recorded history in these islands, there remain to be considered the other strongholds which held the line of the valley.

It would be easy to multiply these if one were to consider all fortifications whatsoever connected with the general strategic line formed by the Thames, but such a catalogue would exceed the boundaries set to this book. It is proposed to consider only those which were strictly connected with the passage of the stream, and of such there are but three besides Dorchester and Oxford, for that at Cricklade is doubtful, and in any case determines a passage which could be always outflanked upon either side, while the great fortress of the Tower, lying as it does upon the estuarial Thames below bridges, does directly protect a highway.

These three strongholds directly connected with the inland river are Wallingford, Reading and Windsor, and of the three Wallingford and Windsor were more directly military: the last, Reading, appears to have been but an adjunct to a large and civil population; the fourfold quality of Reading in the history of the Thames, as a civil settlement, as a religious centre, as a stronghold, and as one of the very few examples of modern industrial development in the valley, will be considered later. We will take each of the three strongholds in their order down stream.

What determined the importance of Wallingford is not easy to fix nowadays. The explanation more usually given to the great part which this crossing of the Thames played in the early history of Britain is the double one that it was the lowest continuously practicable ford over the river, and that it held the passage of the great road going from London to the west.

Now it is true that any traveller making from London to Bath, or the Mendip Hills, and the lower Severn would, on the whole, find his most direct road to be along the Vale of the White Horse, but the convenience of this line through Wallingford may easily be exaggerated, especially its convenience for men in early times before the valleys were properly drained. Though the ford at Abingdon was more difficult than the ford at Wallingford, yet the line through Abingdon westward along the Farringdon road was certainly shorter than the line through Wantage. Whether the old habit, inherited from pre-historic times, of following the chalk ridge had produced a parallel road just at the foot of that ridge and so had made Wallingford, Wantage, and all the southern edge of the Vale of the White Horse the natural road to the west, or whether it was that the great run of travel ran, when once the Thames had been crossed at Wallingford, slightly south-west towards Bath, it is certain that the Wallingford and Wantage line is the line of travel in early history.

There is no record, and but very little basis for conjecture, as to the origin of the fortifications at Wallingford. Not much is left of them, and though there is some Roman work in the place it is work which has evidently been handled over and over again. It is certainly somewhat late in English history that this 'Walled Ford' is heard of – with the tenth century. Its first castle is, of course, Norman, and contemporary with that of Oxford – or rather a year later than that at Oxford, and from the Conquest onward it remains royal. From that time, also, it is perpetually appearing in English history. It was the place of confinement of Edward I when, as Prince Edward, he was the prisoner of Leicester. It was the attempt to succour that prisoner which led to his removal to Kenilworth, and finally to that escape which permitted him to fight the battle of Evesham. Wallingford passed to Gaveston in Edward the Second's reign, and, remaining continually within the gift of the crown, to the Despenser in the succeeding generation, and finally to Isabella, who declared her policy from within the walls of Wallingford when she returned to the country. It was next held by her favourite, Mortimer, and we afterwards find it, throughout the fourteenth century, a sort of appanage of the heir-apparent, and especially of the Duchy of Cornwall, to which it was attached until the Reformation.

It was for a moment under the custody of Chaucer's son: it nursed the childhood of Henry VI, but with the beginning of the next century it had already lost its importance. After half that century had passed the castle was already falling into disrepair; much of the masonry of the town and of the fortress, lying squared and convenient to the river, had been moved down stream for the new buildings at Windsor, and when, nearly a century later again, the Civil War broke out, it was not until after some considerable repair that the place could pretend to stand a siege. It fell to the Parliament, and, before the Restoration, was carefully destroyed, as were throughout England so many foundations of her past by the orders of Oliver Cromwell.

It has often been remarked with surprise that cities and strongholds once densely inhabited and heavily built can disappear and leave no material trace to posterity. That they do so disappear should give pause to those historians who are perpetually using the negative argument, and pretending that the lack of material evidence is sufficient to disturb a strong and early tradition. Those who have watched the process by which abandoned buildings become a quarry will easily understand how all traces of habitation disappear. Three-quarters of what was once Orford, much of what once was Worsted, has gone, and up and down the country-sides to-day one could witness, even in our strictly disciplined civilisation, the removal, by purchase or theft, of abandoned material.

The whole of Wallingford has suffered this fate – the mound, presumably artificial, upon which the first keep stood, and which was, probably, a palisade mound of Anglo-

Saxon times, remains, but there is upon it no remaining masonry.

Next down stream of the points with a strategic importance in English history comes Reading. But the strategic importance of Reading was not produced by the town's possessing a site of national moment: it was produced only by local topography. Reading was never (to use a modern term) a 'nodal point' in the communications of England.

It may be generally laid down that mere strength of position is noted and greedily seized in barbaric times alone. For mere strength of position is a mere refuge. A strong position (I do not speak, of course, of tactical and temporary, but of permanent, positions), chosen only because it is strong, will save you during a critical short period from the attack of a fierce, unthoughtful, and easily wearied enemy – such as are all barbarians; but it cannot *of itself* fall into a general scheme of defence, nor, *simply because it is strong*, intercept the advance of an adversary or support a line of opposition and resistance. Position is always of *advantage* to a fortress, and, in all but highly civilised times, a *necessity* – as we shall see when we come to discuss Windsor – but it is not sufficient. A fortress, when society is organised, and when the feud of one small tribe or family against another is not to be feared, derives its principal value from a command of established communications, and established aggregations of power – especially of economic power. Towns alone can feed and house armies; by roads and railways alone can armies proceed.

There are, indeed, examples of a chain of positions so striking that, from their strength alone, a strategic line imposes itself; but these are very rare. Another, and much commoner, exception to the rule I have stated is the growth of what was once a barbaric stronghold, chosen merely for its position, into a larger centre of population, through which communications necessarily lead, and in which stores and other opportunities for armies can be provided. Such places often preserve a continuity of strategic importance, from civilised, through barbaric, to civilised times again. Laon is an excellent instance of this, and so is Constantine another, and so is Luxembourg a third – indeed they are numerous.

But, in spite of – or, rather, as is proved by – these exceptions the fortresses of an organised people are found at the conjunction of their communications, or at places (such as straits or passes) which have the monopoly of communication, or they are identical with great aggregations of population and opportunity, or at least they are situated in spots from which such aggregations can be commanded. Position is always of value, but only as an adjunct.

Now Reading, save, perhaps, in barbaric times, when the Thames was the main highway of Southern England, occupied no such vantage until the nineteenth century. To-day, with its large population, its provision of steam and electrical power, and above all, its command of the main junction between the southern and middle railways, Reading would again prove of primary strategic importance if we still considered warfare with our equals as a possibility. But during all previous centuries, since the Dark Ages, Reading was potentially, as it is still actually, civilian; and, indeed, it is as the typical great town of the Thames Valley that it will be treated later in these pages.

The long and narrow peninsula between the Kennet and the Thames was an ideal place for defence. It needed but a trench from the one marsh to the other to secure the stronghold. But though this was evident to every fighter, though it is as such a stronghold that Reading is mentioned first in history, yet the advantage was never permanently held. Armies hold Reading, fall back on the town, fight near it, and raid it: but it is never a great fortress in the intervals of wars, because, while Oxford commanded the Drovers' Road, Wallingford the western road, and Windsor (as we shall see in a moment) London itself, Reading neither held a line of supply nor an accumulation of supply, and was, therefore, civilian, though it was nearly as easy to hold as Windsor, as easy as Dorchester, its parallel, easier than Oxford, and far easier than Wallingford, which had, indeed, no natural defences whatsoever.

Proceeding with the stream, there is no further stronghold till we come to Windsor.

Even to-day, and in an England that has lost hold of her past more than has any rival nation, Windsor seems to the passer-by to possess a meaning. That hill of stones, sharp though most of its modern outlines are, set upon another hill for a pedestal, gives, even to a modern patriot, a hint of history; and when it is seen from up-stream, showing its only noble part, where the Middle Ages still linger, it has an aspect almost approaching majesty.

The creator of Windsor was the Conqueror. The artificial mound on which the Round Tower stands may or may not be pre-historic. The slopes of the hill were inhabited, like nearly all our English sites, by the Romans, and by the savages before and after the Romans; but the welter of the Saxon Dark Ages did not use this abrupt elevation for a stronghold. What military reasoning led William of Falaise to discern it at once and there to build his keep?

In order to answer that question let us consider what other points in the valley were at his disposal.

Reading we have discussed. The chalk spurs in the gorge by Goring and Pangbourne are not isolated (as is that of Chateau Gaillard, for instance), and are dominated by the neighbouring heights. The escarpment opposite Henley offered a good site for an eleventh-century castle – but the steep cliff of Windsor had this advantage beyond all the others – that it was at exactly the right distance from London. Windsor is the warden of the capital.

If the reader will look at a modern geological map, he will see from Wallingford to Bray a great belt of chalk in which the trench of the Thames is carved. Alluvials and gravels naturally flank the stream, but chalk is the ground rock of the whole. To the west and to the east of this belt he will notice two curious isolated patches, detached from the main body of the chalk. That to the west forms the twin height of the Sinodun Hills, rising abruptly out of the green sand; that to the east is the knoll of Windsor, rising abruptly out of the thick and damp clay. It is a singular and unique patch, almost exactly round, and as a result of some process at which geology can hardly guess the circle is bisected by the river. If ever the chalk of the north bank rose high it has, in some manner, been worn down. That on the south bank remains in a steep cliff with which everyone who uses the river is familiar. It was the summit of this chalk hill piercing through the clays that the Conqueror noted for his purpose, and he was, to repeat, determined (we must presume) by the distance from London.

The command of a great town, especially a metropolis, is but partially effected by a fortress situated within its limits. In case of a popular revolt, and still more in case the resources of the town are held by an enemy, such a fortress will be penned in and find itself suffering a siege far more rigorous than any that could be laid in an open countryside. On this account the urban fortresses of the Middle Ages are to be found (at least in large cities) lying upon an extreme edge of the walls and reposing, as far as possible, upon uninhabited land or upon water, or both. The two classic examples of this rule are, of course, the Tower and the Louvre, each standing down stream, just outside the wall, and each reposing on the river.

But in an active time even this precaution fails, and that for two reasons. First, the growth of the town makes any possible garrison of the fortress too small for the force with which it might have to cope; and, secondly, this same growth physically overlaps the exterior fortress; suburbs grow up beyond the wall, and the castle finds itself at last embedded in the town. Thus within a hundred and fifty years of its completion the Louvre was but a residence, wholly surrounded, save upon the water front, by the packed houses within the new wall of Marcel.

A tendency therefore arises, more or less early according to local circumstance, to establish a fortified base within striking distance of the civilian centre which it is proposed to command; and striking distance is a day's march. The strict alliance between Paris and the Crown forbade such an experiment to the Capetian Monarchy, but, even in that case, the truth of the general military proposition involved is proved by the power which Montlhéry possessed until the middle of the twelfth century of doing mischief to Paris. In the case of London, and of a population the wealthier of whom were probably for some years hostile to the Conqueror, the immediate necessity for an exterior base presented itself, and though the distance from London was indeed considerable, Windsor, under the circumstances of that moment, proved the most suitable point at which to establish the fortress.

Some centuries earlier or later the exact point for fortification would have lain at *Staines*, and Windsor may be properly regarded as a sort of second best to Staines.

The great Roman roads continued until the twelfth century to be the main highways of the barbaric and mediæval armies. We know, for instance, from a charter of Westminster's, that Oxford Street was called, in the last years of the Saxon Dynasty, 'Via Militaria', and it was this road which was still in its continuation the marching road upon London from the south and west: from Winchester, which was still in a fashion the capital of England and the seat of the Treasury. Now Staines marks the spot where this road crossed the river. It was a 'nodal point', commanding at once the main approach to London by land and the main approach by water.

But there is more than this in favour of Staines. I have already said that a fortress commanding a civilian population

– an ancient fortress, at least – can do so with the best effect at the distance of an easy march. Now Staines is not seventeen miles from Tyburn, and a good road all the way: Windsor is over twenty, and for the last miles there was no good, hard road in the time of its foundation.

But, though Staines had all these advantages, it was rejected from a lack of position. Position was still of first importance, and remained so till the seventeenth century. The new Castle, like so many hundred others built by the genius of the same race, must stand on a steep hill even if the choice of such a site involved a long, instead of a reasonable, day's march. Windsor alone offered that opportunity, and, standing isolated upon the chalk, beyond the tide, accessible by water and by road, became to London what, a hundred years later, Chateau Gaillard was to become for a brief space to Rouen.

The choice was made immediately after the Conquest. In the course of the Dark Ages whatever Roman farms clustered here had dwindled, the Roman cemetery was abandoned, the original name of the district forgotten, and the Saxon 'Winding Shore' grew up at Old Windsor, two or three miles down stream. Old Windsor was not a borough, but it was a very considerable village. It paid dues to its lords to the amount of some twenty-five loads of corn and more – say 100 quarters – and it had at least 100 houses, since that number is set down in Domesday, and, as we have previously said, Domesday figures necessarily express a minimum. We may take it that its population was something in the neighbourhood of 1000.

This considerable place was under the lordship of the

abbots of Westminster. It had been a royal manor when Edward the Confessor came to the throne; he gave it to his new great abbey. When the Conqueror needed the whole neighbourhood for his new purpose he exchanged it against land in Essex, which he conveyed to the abbey, and he added (for the manorial system was still flexible) half a hide from Clewer on the west side of the Windsor territory. This half-hide gave him his approach to the platform of chalk on which he designed to build.

He began his work quickly. Within four years of Hastings, and long before the conquest of the Saxon aristocracy was complete, he held his Court at Windsor and summoned a synod there, and, though we do not know when the keep was completed, we can conjecture, from the rapidity with which all Norman work was done, that the walls were defensible even at that time. Of his building perhaps nothing remains. The forest to the south, with its opportunities for hunting, and the increasing importance of London (which was rapidly becoming the capital of England) made Windsor of greater value than ever in the eyes of his son. Henry I rebuilt or greatly enlarged the castle, lived in it, was married in it, and accomplished in it the chief act of his life, when he caused fealty to be sworn to his daughter, Matilda, and prepared the advent of the Angevin. When the civil wars were over, and the treaty between Henry II and Stephen was signed, Windsor ('Mota de Windsor'), though it does not seem to have stood a siege, was counted the second fortress of the realm.

Of the exact place of Windsor in mediæval strategy, of its relations to London and to Staines, and all we have just mentioned, as also of the great importance of cavalry in the Middle Ages, no better example can be quoted than the connected episode of April–June 1215, which may be called – to give it a grandiose name – the Campaign of Magna Charta. It further illustrates points which should never be forgotten in the reading of early English history, though they are too particular for the general purpose of this book – to wit, the way in which London increased in military value throughout the twelfth and thirteenth centuries; the strategic importance of the few old national roads as late as the reign of John, and that power of the defensive, even in the field, which made general and strategic, as opposed to tactical, attack so cautious, decisive action so rare, and when it *was* decisive, so thorough.

This book is no place wherein to develop a theme which history will confirm with regard to the aristocratic revolt against the vice and the genius of the third Plantagenet. The strategy of the quarrel alone concerns us.

When John's admirable diplomacy had failed (as diplomacy will under the test of arms), and when his Continental allies had been crushed at Bouvines in the summer of 1214, the rebels in England found their opportunity. The great lords, especially those of the north, took oath in the autumn to combine. The accounts of this conspiracy are imperfect, but its general truth may be accepted. John, who from this moment lay perpetually behind walls, held a conference in the Temple during the January of 1215 – to be accurate, upon the Epiphany of that year – and he struck a compact with the conspirators that there should be a truce between their forces and those of the Crown until Low Sunday – which fell that year upon 26 April. The great nobles, mistrusting his faith with some justice (especially as he had taken the Cross), gathered their army some ten days before the expiry of the interval, but, as befitted men who claimed in especial to defend the Catholic Church and its principles, they were scrupulous not to engage in actual fighting before the appointed day. The size of this army we cannot tell, but as it contained from 2000 to 3000 armed and mounted gentlemen it must have counted at least double that tale of cavalry, and perhaps five-, perhaps ten-fold the number of foot soldiers. A force of 15,000 to 30,000 men in an England of some 5 million (I more than double the conventional figures) was prepared to enforce feudal independence against the central government, even at the expense of ceding vast territories to Scotland or of submitting to the nominal rule of a foreign king. Against this army the King had a number of mercenaries, mainly drawn from his Continental possessions, probably excellent soldiers, but scattered among the numerous garrisons which it was his titular office to defend.

In the last days of the truce the rebels marched to Brackley and encamped there on Low Monday – 27 April. The choice of the site should be noted. It lies in a nexus of several old marching roads. The Port Way, a Roman road from Dorchester northward, the Watling Street all lay within half-an-hour's ride. The King was at Oxford, a day's march away. They negotiated with him, and their claims were refused, yet they did not attack him (though his force was small), partly because the function of government was still with him and partly because the defensive power of Oxford was great. They wisely preferred the nearest of his small official garrisons – that holding the castle of Northampton. They approached it up the Roman road through Towcester. They failed before it after two weeks of effort, and marched on to the next royal post at Bedford, which was by far the nearest of the national garrisons. It was betrayed to them. When they were within the gates they received a message from the wealthier citizens of London (who were in practice one with the Feudal Oligarchy), begging them to enter the capital.

What followed could only have been accomplished by cavalry, by cavalry in high training, by a force under excellent generalship, and by one whose leaders appreciated the all-importance of London in the coming struggle. The rebels left Bedford immediately, marched all that day, all the succeeding night, and early on the Sunday morning, 24 May, entered London, and by the northern gate. Their entry was not even challenged.

From Bedford to St Paul's is – as the crow flies – between forty and fifty miles: whatever road a man may take would make it nearer fifty than forty. Bearing, as did this army, towards the east until it struck the Ermine Street, the whole march must have been well over fifty miles.

This fine feat was not a barren one: it was well worth the effort and loss which it must have cost. London could feed, recruit, and remount an army of even this magnitude with ease. The Tower was held by a royal garrison, but it could do nothing against so great a town.

From London, as though the name of the city had a

sort of national authority, the Barons, who now felt themselves to be hardly rebels but almost co-equals in a civil
war, issued letters of mandate to others of their class and
to their inferiors. These letters were obeyed, not perhaps
without some hesitation, but at any rate with a final obedience which turned the scale against the King. John was
now in a very distinct inferiority, and even of his personal
attendants a considerable number left the Court on learning
of the defection of London. In all this long struggle nothing but the occupation of the capital had proved enough to
make John feign a compromise. As excellent an intriguer as
he was a fighter he asked nothing better than to hear once
more the terms of the Barons.

He proceeded to *Windsor*, asked for a parley, issued a
safeguard to the emissaries of the Barons, and despatched
this document upon 8 June, giving it a validity of three
days. His enemies waited somewhat longer, perhaps in
order to collect the more distant contingents, and named
Runnymede – a pasture upon the right bank of the Thames
just above *Staines* – as the place of meeting.

There are those who see in the derivation of the name
'Runnymede' an ancient use of the meadow as a place of
council. This is, of course, mere conjecture, but at any rate
it was, at this season of the year, a large, dry field, in which
a considerable force could encamp. The Barons marched
along the old Roman military road, which is still the
high-road to Staines from London, crossed the river, and
encamped on Runnymede. Here the Charta was presented,
and probably, though not certainly, signed and sealed. The
local tradition ascribes the site of the actual signature to

'Magna Charta' island – an eyot just up-stream from the field, now called Runnymede, but neither in tradition nor in recorded history can this detail be fixed with any exactitude. The Charta is given as from Runnymede upon 15 June, and for the purpose of these pages what we have to note is that these two months of marching and fighting had ended upon the strategic point of Staines, and had clearly shown its relation to Windsor and to London.

In the short campaign that followed, during which John so very nearly recovered his power, the capital importance of Windsor reappears. Louis of France, to whom the Barons were willing to hand over what was left of order in England, had occupied all the south and west, including even Worcester, and, of course, London. In this occupation the exception of Dover, which the French were actively besieging, must be regarded as an isolated point, but *Windsor*, which John's men held against the allies, threw an angle of defence right down into the midst of the territory lost to the Crown. Windsor was, of course, besieged; but John's garrison, holding out as it did, saved the position. The King was at Wallingford at one moment during the siege; his proximity tempted the enemy to raise the siege, to leave Windsor in the hands of the royal garrison, and to advance against him, or rather to cut him off in his advance eastward. They marched with the utmost rapidity to Cambridge, but John was ahead of them: and before they could return to the capture of Windsor he was rapidly confirming his power in the north and the east.

It must not be forgotten in all this description that Windsor was helped in its development as a fortress by the presence to the south of the hill of a great space of waste lands.

These waste lands of Western Europe, which it was impossible or unprofitable to cultivate, were, by a sound political tradition, vested in the common authority, which was the Crown.

Indeed they still remain so vested in most European countries. The Cantons of Switzerland, the Communes and the National Governments of France, Italy, and Spain remain in possession of the waste. It is only with us that wealthy private owners have been permitted to rob the Commonwealth of so obvious an inheritance, a piece of theft which they have accomplished with complete cynicism, and by specific acts whose particular dates can be quoted, though historians are very naturally careful to leave the process but vaguely analysed. Indeed, the last and most valuable of these waste spaces, the New Forest itself, might have entirely disappeared had not Charles I (the last king in England to attempt a repression of the landed class) so forcibly urged the local engrosser to disgorge as to compel him, with Hampden and the rest, to a burning zeal for political liberty.

This great waste space to the south of Windsor Hill became, after the Conquest, the Forest, and apart from the hunting which it afforded to the Royal palace, served a certain purpose on the military side as well.

To develop a thought which has already been touched on in these pages, mediæval fortification was dual in character: it had either a purely strategical object, in which case the site was chosen with an eye to its military value, whether inhabited or not, or the stronghold or fortification was made to develop an already existing town or site of importance. Of the second sort was Wallingford, but of the first sort, as we have seen, was Windsor. Indeed the distinction is normal to all fortification and exists upon the Continent to-day. For instance, the first-class fortress Paris is an example of the second sort, the first-class fortress Toul of the first. Again, all German fortresses, without exception, are of the second sort, while all Swiss fortification, what little of it exists, is of the first.

Now where the first category is concerned a waste space is of value, though its dimensions will vary in military importance according to the means of communication of the time. A stronghold may be said to repose upon that side through which communications are most difficult.

It is true that this space lying to the south of Windsor was of no very great dimensions, but such as it was, uninhabited and therefore unprovided with stores of any kind, it prevented surprise from the south.

The next point of strategic importance on the Thames, and the last, is the Tower.

Though it is below bridges it must fall into the scheme of this book, because its whole military history and connection with the story of England is bound up with the inland and not with the estuarial river.

It was, as has already been pointed out, one long day's march from Windsor – a march along the old Roman road from Staines. This land passage more than halved the distance by river, it cut off not only the numerous large turns which the Thames begins to take between Middlesex and Surrey, but also the general sweep southward of the river, and it avoided, what another road might have necessitated, the further crossing of the stream.

Long as the march is, there was no fortification of importance between one point and the other, and mediæval history is crammed with instances of armies leaving the Tower to march to Windsor in one day, or leaving Windsor to march to the Tower.

The position of the Tower we saw in an earlier page to be due to the same geographical causes as had built up so many of the urban strongholds of Europe. It was situated upon the very bank of the river which fed the capital, it was down stream from the town, and it was just outside the walls. In a word, it was the parallel of the Louvre.

Its remote origins are doubtful; some have imagined that they are Roman, and that if not in the first part of the Roman occupation at least towards the end of those wealthy and populous three centuries, which are the foundation and the making of England, some fortification was built on the brow of the little eminence which here slopes down to the high-water mark.

I will quote the evidence, such as it is, and the reader will perceive how difficult it is to arrive at a conclusion.

Of actual Roman remains all we have is a couple of coins of the end of the fourth century (probably minted at Constantinople), a silver ingot of the same period, and a funeral inscription. No indubitably Roman work has been discovered.

On the other hand there has been no modern investigation of those foundations of the White Tower where, if

anywhere, Roman work might be expected. This exhausts
the direct evidence. In sciences such as geology or the
criticism of Sacred Books evidence to this extent would
be ample to overset the firmest traditions or the most
self-evident conclusion of common human experience. But
history is bound to a greater caution, and it must be reluc-
tantly admitted that the two coins, the ingot and the bit
of stone are insufficient to prove the existence of a Roman
fortress.

Leaving such material and direct evidence we have the
tradition, which is a fairly strong one, of Roman fortification here, and we have the analogy, so frequently occur-
ring in space and time throughout the history and the area
of Western Europe, that Gaul reproduces Rome. What
the Conqueror saw (it might be vaguely argued) to be the
strategical position for London, that a Roman emperor
would have seen. But against this argument from tradition,
which is fairly strong, and that argument from analogy,
which is weak, we have other and contrary considerations.

Rome even in her decline did not build her citadels
outside the walls: that was a habit which grew up in the
Dark and early Middle Ages, and was attached to the differ-
entiation between the civic and military aspects of the
State.

Again, Roman fortification of every kind is connected
with earthworks. So far as we can tell from recorded
history the ditch round the Tower was not dug till the end
of the twelfth century. Finally, there is this strong argument against the theory of a Roman origin to the Tower
that had such a Roman fortress existed an extension of the

town would almost certainly have gathered round it.

One of the features of the break-up of Roman society was the enormous expansion of the towns. We have evidence of it on every side and nowhere more than in Northern Africa. This expansion took place everywhere, but especially and invariably in the presence of a garrison, and indeed the military conditions of the fourth century, with its cosmopolitan and partially hereditary army, fixed in permanent garrisons and forming as it were a local caste, presupposed a large dependent civilian population at the very gates of the camp or stronghold. Thus you have the Palatine suburb to the south of Lutetia right up against the camp, and Verecunda just outside Lamboesis. Now there is nothing of the sort in the neighbourhood of the Tower. It seems certain that from the earliest times London ended here cleanly at the wall, and that except along the Great Eastern Road the neighbourhood of the Tower was agricultural land.

How then could a tradition have arisen with regard to Roman occupation? It is but a conjecture, though a plausible one, that when the pirate raids grew in severity this knoll down stream was fortified, while still the ruling class was Latin speaking and while still the title of Cæsar was familiar, whether before or after the withdrawal of the Legions. If this were the case, then, on the analogy of other similar sites, one may imagine something like the following: that in the Dark Ages the masonry was used as a quarry for other constructions, that the barbarians would occasionally stockade the site, though not permanently, and only for the purposes of their ephemeral but constant quarrels; and one may suggest that when the barbaric period was ended, by the landing of William's army, the place was still, by a tradition now six hundred years old, a public area under the control of the Crown and one such as would lend itself to the design of a permanent fortification. William, finding it in this condition, erected upon it the great keep which was to be the last of his fortifications along the line of the river, and the pivot for the control of London.

This keep is of course the White Tower, which still impresses even our generation with the squat and square shoulders of Norman strength. It and Ely are the best remaining expressions of the hardy little men, and it fills one, as does everything Norman, from the Tyne to the Euphrates, with something of awe. This building, the White Tower, is the Tower itself; the rest is but an accretion, partly designed for defence, but latterly more for habitation. Its name of the 'White' Tower is probably original, though we do not actually find the term 'La Blaunche Tour' till near the middle of the fourteenth century. The presumption that it is the original name is founded upon a much earlier record – namely, that of 1241, in which not only is it ordered that the tower be repainted white, but in which mention is also made that its original colour had been 'worn by the weather and by the long process of time'. Such a complaint would take one back to the twelfth century, and quite probably to the first building of the Keep. The object of whitening the walls of the Tower is again explicable by the very reasonable conjecture that it would so serve as a landmark over the long, flat stretches of the lower river. It was the last conspicuous building against the mass of the great town, and there are many examples of similar landmarks used at the head of estuaries or sea passages. When these are not spires they are almost invariably white, especially where they are so situated as to catch the southern or the eastern sun.

The exact date at which the plan was undertaken we do not know, but it is obviously one with the scheme of building Windsor, and must date from much the same period. The order to build was given by the Conqueror to the Bishop of Rochester, Gundulph. Now Gundulph was not promoted to the See of Rochester till 1077. Exactly twenty years later, in 1097, the son of the Conqueror built the outer wall. The Keep was then presumed to be completed, and at some time during those twenty years it must have been begun, probably about 1080. That which we have seen increasing, the military importance of Windsor, diminished the military importance of the Tower, until, with the close of the Middle Ages, it had become no more than a prison. It was not indeed swamped by the growth of the town, as was its parallel the Louvre, but the increase of wealth (and therefore of the means of war), coupled with the correspondingly increased population, made both urban fortresses increasingly difficult to hold as mediæval civilisation developed.

The whole history of the Tower is the history of military misfortune, which grows as London expands in numbers and prosperity. It probably held out under Mandeville when the Londoners (who were always the allies of the aristocracy against the national government) besieged it under the civil wars of Stephen; but even so there was bad luck attached to it, for when Mandeville was taken prisoner he was compelled to sign its surrender. Within a generation Longchamp again surrendered it to the young Prince John; he was for the moment leading the aristocracy, which, when it was his turn to reign, betrayed him. It was surrendered to the baronial party by the King as a trust or pledge for the execution of Magna Charta, and though it was put into the hands of the Archbishop, who was technically neutral, it was from that moment the symbol of a successful rebellion, as it had already proved to be in the past and was to prove so often again.

It was handed over to Louis of France upon his landing, and during the next reign almost every misfortune of Henry III is connected with the Tower. He was perpetually taking refuge in it, holding his Court in it: losing it again, as the rebels succeeded, and regaining it as they failed. This long and unfortunate tenure of his is illumined only by one or two delightful phrases which one cannot but retain as one reads. Thus there is the little written order, which still remains to us for the putting of painted windows into the Chapel of St John, the northern one of which was to have for its design 'some little Mary or other, holding her Child' – 'quandam Mariolam tenenten puerum suum'. There is also a very pleasing legend in the same year, 1241, when the fall of certain new buildings was ascribed to the action of St Thomas, who was seen by a priest in a dream upsetting them with his crozier and saying that he did this 'as a good citizen of London, because these new buildings were not put up for the defence of the realm but to overawe the town', and he added this charming remark: 'If I had not undertaken the duty myself St Edward or another would have done it.'

Even when Henry's misfortunes were at an end, and when the Battle of Evesham was won, the Tower was perpetually unfortunate. A body of rebels surrounded it, and in the defence were present a great number of Jews, who had fled from the fighting in the city only to find themselves pressed for service in defence of the fortress. From that moment they make no further appearance in English military history till the South African War, unless indeed their appearance in chains thirteen years later in this same Tower as prisoners for financial trickery can be counted a military event.

Upon this occasion the siege was raised by the promptitude and energy of Prince Edward – the man who as King was to march to Cærnarvon and to the Grampians had already in his boyhood shown the energy and the military aptitude of his grandfather King John. He was but twenty years old, yet he had already done all the fighting at Lewes, he had already won Evesham, and now, at the end of spring, he made one march from Windsor to the Tower and relieved it. It was almost the last time that the Tower stood for the success of authority. From this time onwards it is, as it had been before, the unfortunate symbol of successful rebellion. Edward II had to leave it in his fatal year of 1326, the Londoners poured in and incidentally massacred the Bishop of Exeter, into whose hands it had been entrusted.

In 1460 it surrendered to the House of York, and from that time onwards becomes more and more of a prison and less and less of a fortress.

The preponderatingly military aspect of the Thames Valley in English history dwindles with the dwindling of military energy in our civilisation, and passes with the passing of a governing class that was military rather than commercial.

Sites which owed their importance to strategical position, and which had hence grown into considerable towns, ceased to show any but a civilian character, and even in the only episode of consequence wherein fighting occurred in England since the Middle Ages – the episode of the Civil Wars – the banks of the Thames, though perpetually infested by either army, saw very little serious fighting, and that although the line of the Thames was the critical line of action during the first stage of the war.

For the Civil Wars as a whole were but an affair upon the flank of the general struggle in Europe: the losses were never heavy, and in the first stages one can hardly call it fighting at all.

The losses at the skirmish of Edge Hill were, indeed, respectable, though most of them seem to have been incurred after the true fighting ceased, but with that exception, and especially upon the line of the Thames itself, the losses were extraordinarily small.

One may say that Oxford and London were the two objective points of the opposing forces from the close of 1642 to the spring of 1644. The King's Government at Oxford, the Parliament in London, were the civil bases, at least, upon which the opposing forces pivoted, and the two intermediate points were Abingdon and Reading. To read the contemporary, and even the modern, history of the time, one would imagine from the terms used that these places were the theatre of considerable military operations. We hear, with every technicality which the Continental struggle had rendered familiar to Englishmen, of sieges, assaults, headquarters, and even hornworks. But when one looks at dates and figures it is not easy to treat the matter seriously. Here, for instance, is Abingdon, within a short walk of Oxford, and the Royalists easily allow it to be occupied by Essex in the spring of '44. Even so Abingdon is not used as a base for doing anything more serious than 'molesting' the university town. And it was so held that Rupert tried to recapture it, of all things in the world, with cavalry! He was 'overwhelmed' by the vastly superior forces of the enemy, and his attempt failed. When one has thoroughly grasped this considerable military event one next learns that the overwhelming forces were a trifle over a thousand in number!

Next an individual gentleman with a few followers conceives the elementary idea of blocking the western road at Culham Bridge, and isolating Abingdon upon this side. He begins building a 'fort'. A certain proportion of the handful in Abingdon go out and kill him and the fort is not proceeded with: and so forth. A military temper of this sort very easily explains the cold-blooded massacre of prisoners which the Parliament permitted, and which has given to the phrase 'Abingdon Law' the unpleasant flavour which it still retains.

The story of Reading in the earlier part of the struggle is much the same. Reading was held as a royal garrison and fortified in '43. According to the garrison the fortification was contemptible, according to the procedures it was of the most formidable kind. Indeed they doubted whether it could be captured by an assault of less than 5000 men, a number which appeared at this stage of the campaign so appalling that it is mentioned as a sort of standard of comparison with the impossible. The garrison surrendered just as relief was approaching it, and after a strain which it had endured for no less than ten days; but the capture of Reading was not effected entirely without bloodshed; certainly fifty men were killed (counting both sides), possibly a few more; and the whole episode is a grotesque little foot-note to the comic opera upon which rose the curtain of the Civil Wars. It was not till the appearance of Cromwell, with his highly paid and disciplined force, that the tragedy began.

Even after Cromwell had come forward as the chief leader, in fact if not in name, the apparent losses are largely increased by the random massacres to which his soldiers were unfortunately addicted. Thus after Naseby a hundred women were killed for no particular reason except that killing was in the air, and similarly after Philiphaugh the conscience of the Puritans forbade them to keep their word to the prisoners they had taken, who were put to the sword in cold blood: the women, however, on this occasion, were drowned.

After the Civil Wars all the military meaning of the Thames disappears. Nor is it likely to revive short of a national disaster; but that disaster would at once teach us the strategical meaning of this great highway running through the south of England with its attendant railways, it would re-create the strategical value of the point where the Thames turns northward and where its main railways bifurcate; it would provide in several conceivable cases, as it provided to Charles I and to William III, the line of approach on London.

℘

So far as we have considered the Thames, first as a line of pre-historic settlements, passing successively into the Roman, the barbaric and the Norman phases of our history; and secondly, as a field on which one can plot out certain strategical points and show how these points created the original importance of the towns which grew about them.

In the next part of these notes I propose to consider the economic or civil development of the Thames above London, and to show how the foundations of its permanent prosperity was laid. That economic phenomenon has at its roots the action of the Benedictine Order. It was the great monasteries which bridged the transition between Rome and the Dark Ages throughout North-Western Europe; it was they that recovered land wasted by the barbarian invasions, and that developed heaths and fens which the Empire even in its maturity had never attempted to exploit.

The effect of the barbarian invasions was different in different provinces of the Roman Empire, though roughly speaking it increased in intensity with the distance from Rome. It is probable that the actual numbers of the barbarian invaders was small even in Britain, as it certainly was in Northern Gaul, but we must not judge of the effect produced upon civilisation by this catastrophe, as though it were a mere question of numbers. So large a proportion of the population was servile, and so fixed had the imagination of everyone become in the idea that the social order was eternal; so entirely had the army become a professional thing, and probably a thing of routine divorced from the civilian life round it, that at the close of the fourth century a little shock from without was enough to produce a very considerable result. In Eastern Britain, small as the number of the invaders must necessarily have been, religion itself was almost, if not entirely, destroyed, and the whole fabric of Roman civilisation appears to have dissolved – with the exception, of course, of such irremovable things as the agricultural system, the elements of municipal life, and the simpler arts. Even the language very probably changed in the eastern part of the island, and passed from what we may conceive to have been Low Latin in the towns and Celtic dialects in the country-sides, with possibly Teutonic settlements here and there along the eastern shore, to a generally confused mass of Teutonic dialects scattered throughout the eastern and northern half of the island and enclosing but isolated fragments of Celtic speech.

So far as we can judge the disaster was complete, but it was destined that Britain should be recivilised.

St Augustine landed, and after the struggle of the seventh century between those petty chieftains who sympathised with, and those who opposed, the order of cultivated European life, the battle was won in favour of that civilisation which we still enjoy. It would have been impossible to re-create a sound agriculture and to refound the arts and learning; especially would it have been impossible to refound the study of letters, upon which all material civilisation depends, had it not been for the monastic institution. This institution did more work in Britain than in any other province of the Empire. And it had far more to do. It found a district utterly wrecked, perhaps half depopulated, and having lost all but a vague memory of the old Roman order;

it had to remake, if it could, of all this part of a Europe. No other instrument was fitted for the purpose.

The chief difficulty of starting again the machine of civilisation when its parts have been distorted by a barbarian interlude, whether external or internal in origin, is the accumulation of capital. The next difficulty is the preservation of such capital in the midst of continual petty feuds and raids, and the third is that general continuity of effort, and that treasuring up of proved experience, to which a barbaric time, succeeding upon the decline of a civilisation, is particularly unfitted. For the surmounting of all these difficulties the monks of Western Europe were suited to a high degree. Fixed wealth could be accumulated in the hands of communities whose whole temptation was to gather, and who had no opportunity for spending in waste. The religious atmosphere in which they grew up forbade their spoliation, at least in the internal wars of a Christian people, and each of the great foundations provided a community of learning and treasuring up of experience which single families, especially families of barbaric chieftains, could never have achieved. They provided leisure for literary effort, and a strict disciplinary rule enforcing regular, continuous, and assiduous labour, and they provided these in a society from which exact application of such a kind had all but disappeared.

The monastic institution, so far as Western Europe was concerned, was comparatively young when the work in Britain was begun. The fifth century had seen its inception; it was still embryonic in the sixth; the seventh, which was the date of its great conquest of the English country-sides, was for it a period of youth and of vigour as fresh as was, let us say, the thirteenth century for the renaissance of civil learning. We must not think of these early foundations as we think of the complicated, wealthy, somewhat restricted and privileged bodies of the later Middle Ages. They were all more or less of one type, and that type a simple one. They all sprang from the same Benedictine stem. It was the quality of all to be somewhat independent in management, and especially to work in large units, and out of the very many which sprang up all over the island three particularly concern the Thames Valley. Each of them dates from the very beginnings of Anglo-Saxon history, each of them has its roots in legend, and each of them continued for close upon a thousand years to be a capital economic centre of English life. These three great Benedictine foundations are WESTMINSTER, CHERTSEY, and ABINGDON.

When civilisation returned in fullness with the Norman Conquest, another great house of the first importance was founded – at Reading; and, much later, a fourth at Sheen. To these we shall turn in their place, as also to the string of dependent houses and small foundations which line the river almost from its source right down to London: indeed the only type of religious foundation which historic notes such as these can afford to neglect is the monastery or nunnery built in a town, and for the purposes of a town, after the civic life of a town had developed. These very numerous houses (most numerous, of course, in Oxford), such as the Observants of Richmond and a host of others, do not properly enter into the scheme we are considering. They are not causes but effects of the development of civilisation in the Thames Valley.

Abingdon, Westminster, and Chertsey are all ascribed by tradition, and each by a very vital and well-documented tradition, to the seventh century: Abingdon and Chertsey to its close; Westminster, with less assurance, to its beginning. All three, we may take it, did arise in that period which was for the eastern part of this island a time when all the work of Europe had to be begun again. Though we know nothing of the progress of the Saxon pirates in the province of Britain, and though history is silent for the hundred and fifty years covered by the disaster, yet on the analogy of other and later raids from the North Sea we may imagine that no inland part of the country suffered more than the valley of the Thames. All that was left of the Roman order, wealth and right living, must have appeared at the close of that sixth century, when the Papal Mission landed, something as appears the wrecked and desolate land upon the retirement of a flood. To cope with such conditions, to reintroduce into the ravaged and desecrated province, which had lost its language in the storm, all its culture, and even its religion, a new beginning of energy and of production came, with the peculiar advantages we have seen it to possess for such a work, the monastic institution. For two centuries the great houses were founded all over England: their attachment to Continental learning, their exactitude, their corporate power of action, were all in violent contrast to, and most powerfully educational for, the barbarians in the midst of whom they grew. It may be truly said that if we regard the life of England as beginning anew with the Saxon invasion, if that disaster of the pirate raids be considered as so great that it offers a breach of continuity in the history of Britain, then the new country which sprang up, speaking Teutonic dialects, and calling itself by its present name of England, was actually created by the Benedictine monks.

It was within a very few years of St Augustine's landing that Westminster must have been begun. There are several versions of the story: the most detailed statement we have ascribes it to the particular year 604, but varied as are the forms in which the history, or rather the legend, is preserved, the truth common to all is the foundation quite early in the seventh century. It was very probably supported by what barbaric Government there was in London at the time and initiated, moreover, according to one form of the legend, and that not the least plausible, by the first bishop of the see. The site was at the moment typical of all those which the great monasteries of the West were to turn from desert places to gardens: it was a waste tract of ground called 'Thorney', lying low, triangular in shape, bounded by the two reedy streams that descended through the depression which now runs across the Green Park and Mayfair, and emptied themselves into the Thames, the one just above, the other 100 or 200 yards below, the site of the Houses of Parliament.

The moment the foundation was established a stream of wealth tended towards it: it was at the very gate of the largest commercial city in the kingdom and it was increasingly associated, as the Anglo-Saxon monarchy developed, with the power of the Central Government. This process culminated in the great donation and rebuilding of Edward the Confessor.

The period of this new endowment was one well chosen to launch the future glory of Westminster. England was all prepared to be permeated with the Norman energy, and when immediately after the Conquest came, the great shrine inherited all the glamour of a lost period, while it established itself with the new power as a sort of symbol of the continuity of the Crown. There William was anointed, there was his palace and that of his son. When, with the next century, the seat of Government became fixed, and London was finally established as the capital, Westminster had already become the seat of the monarchy.

Chertsey, next up the river, took on the work. Like Westminster – though, by tradition, a few years later than Westminster – its foundation goes back to the birth of England. Its history is known in some detail, and is full of incident, so that it may be called the pivot upon which, presumably, turned the development of the Thames Valley above London for two hundred years. Its site is worth noting. The rich, but at first probably swampy, pasturage upon the Surrey side was just such a position as one foundation after another up and down England settled on. To reclaim land of this kind was one of the special functions of the great abbeys, and Chertsey may be compared in this particular to Hyde, for instance, or to the Vale of the Cross, to Fountains, to Ripon, to Melrose, and to many others. It was in the new order of monastic development what Staines, its neighbour, had been in the old Roman order – the mark of the first stage up-river from London.

The pagan storm which all but repeated in Britain the disaster of the Saxon invasions, which all but overcame the mystic tenacity of Alfred and the positive mission of the town of Paris, swept it completely. Its abbot and its ninety monks were massacred, and it was not till late in the next century, about 950, that it arose again from its ruins. It was deliberately re-colonised again from Abingdon, and from that moment onwards it grew again into power. Donations poured upon it; one of them, not the least curious, was of land in Cardiganshire. It came from those Welsh princes who were perpetually at war with the English Crown: for religion was in those days what money is now – a thing without frontiers – and it seemed no more wonderful to the Middle Ages that an English monastery should collect its rents in an enemy's land than it seems strange to us that the modern financier should draw interest upon money lent for armament against the country of his domicile. Here also was first buried (and lay until it was removed to Windsor) the body of Henry VI.

The third of the great early foundations is Abingdon, and in a way it is the greatest, for, without direct connection with the Crown, by the mere vitality of its tradition, it became something more even than Chertsey was, wielding an immense revenue, more than half that of Westminster itself, and situated, as it was, in a small up-valley town, ruling with almost monarchical power. There could be even less doubt in the case of Abingdon than there was in the case of Chertsey that it was the creator of its own district of the Thames. It stood right in the marshy and waste spaces of the middle upper river, commanding a difficult but an important ford, and holding the gate of what was to be one of the most fruitful and famous of English vales. It can only have been from Abingdon that the culture and energy proceeded which was to build up Northern Berkshire and Oxfordshire between the Saxon and the Danish invasions. There only was established a sufficient concentration of capital for the work and of knowledge for the application of that wealth.

Like its two peers at Chertsey and at Westminster, Abingdon begins with legend. We are fairly sure of its date, 675, but the anchorite of the fifth century, 'Aben', is as suspicious as the early Anglo-Saxon Chronicle itself, and still wilder are the fine and striking stories of its British origin, of its destruction under the persecution of Diocletian and of its harbouring the youth of Constantine. But the stories are at least enough to show with what violence the pomp and grandeur of the place struck the imagination of its historians.

Abingdon was, moreover, probably on account of its distance from London, more of a local centre, and, to repeat a word already used, more of a 'monarchy' than the other great monasteries of the Thames Valley. This is sufficiently proved by a glance at the ecclesiastic map, such as, for instance, that published in 'The Victoria History of the County of Berkshire', where one sees the manors belonging to Abingdon at the time of the Conquest all clustered together and occupying one full division of the county, that, namely, included in the great bend of the Thames which has its cusp at Witham Hill. Abingdon was the life of Northern Berkshire, and it is not fantastic to compare its religious aspect in Saxon times over against the King's towns of Wantage and Wallingford to the larger national aspect of

Canterbury over against Winchester and London.

Even in its purely civic character, it acquired a position which no one of the greater northern monasteries could pretend to, through the building of its bridge in the early fifteenth century. The twin fords crossing this bend of the river were, though direct and important, difficult; when they were once bridged and the bridges joined by the long causeway which still runs across Andersey Island between the old and the new branches of the Thames, travel was easily diverted from the bridge of Wallingford to that at Abingdon, and the great western road running through Farringdon towards the Cotswolds and the valley of the Severn had Abingdon for its sort of midway market town.

These three great Benedictine monasteries form, as it were, the three nurseries or seed plots from which civilisation spread out along the Thames Valley after the destruction wrought by the first and worst barbarian invasions. All three, as we have seen, go back to the very beginning of the Christian phase of English history; the origins of all three merge in those legends which make a twilight between the fantastic stories of the earlier paganism and the clear records of the Christian epoch after the re-Latinisation of England. An outpost beyond these three is the institution of St Frideswides at Oxford. Beyond that point the upper river, gradually narrowing, losing its importance for commerce and as a highway, supported no great monastery, and felt but tardily the economic change wrought by the foundations lower down the stream.

Chertsey and Westminster certainly, and Abingdon very probably, were destroyed, or at least sacked, in the

Danish invasions, but their roots lay too deep to allow them to disappear: they re-arose, and a generation before the Conquest were again by far the principal centres of production and government in the Thames Valley. Indeed, with the exception of the string of royal estates upon the banks of the river, and of the town of Oxford, Chertsey, Westminster and Abingdon were the only considerable seats of regulation and government upon the Thames, when the Conquest came to reorganise the whole of English life.

With that revolution it was evident that a great extension not only of the numbers, but especially of the organisation and power, of the monastic system would appear: that gaps left uninfluenced by it in the line of the Thames would be filled up, and all the old foundations themselves would be reconstructed and become new things.

The Conquest is in its way almost as sharp a division in the history of England as is the landing of St Augustine. In some externals it made an even greater difference to this island than did the advent of the Roman Missionaries, though of course, in the fundamental things upon which the national life is built, the re-entry of England into European civilisation in the seventh century must count as a far greater and more decisive event than its first experience of united and regular government under the Normans in the eleventh. Moreover although the Conquest largely changed the language of the island, introduced a conception of law in civil affairs with which the Anglo-Saxon aristocracy were quite unfamiliar, and began to flood England with a Gallic admixture which flowed uninterruptedly for three hundred years, yet it did not change the intimate philosophy of the people, and it is only the change of the intimate philosophy of a people which can have a revolutionary consequence. The Conquest found England Catholic, vaguely feudal, and, though in rather an isolated way, thoroughly European. The Normans organised that feudality, extirpated whatever was unorthodox, or slack in the machinery of the religious system, and let in the full light of European civilisation through a wide-open door, which had hitherto been half-closed.

The effect, therefore, of the Conquest was exercised upon the visible and mutable things of the country rather than upon the nourishing inward things: but it was very great, and in nothing was it greater than in its inception of new buildings and the use everywhere of stone. Under the Normans very nearly all the great religious foundations of England re-arose, and that within a generation. New houses also arose, and the mark of that time (which was a second spring throughout Europe: full of the spirit of the Crusades, and a complete regeneration of social life) was the rigour of new religious orders, and especially the transformation of the old Benedictine monotony.

Chief, of course, of these religious movements, and the pioneer of them all, was the institution of Cluny in Burgundy.

Cluny did not rise by design. It was one of those spontaneous growths which are characteristic of vigorous and creative times. Those who are acquainted with the Burgundian blood will not think it fantastic to imagine the vast reputation of Cluny to have been based upon rhetoric. It was perhaps the sonorous Burgundian facility for expression and the inheritance of oratory which belonged to Burgundian soil till Bossuet's birth, and which still belongs to it, that gave Cluny a sort of spell over the mind of Western Europe, and which made Cluny a master in the century which preceded the great change of the Crusades. From Cluny as a mother house proceeded communities instinct with the discipline and new life of the reformed order, and though it has been remarked that these communities were not numerous, in comparison to the vigour of the movement, yet it should also be noted that they were nearly always very large and wealthy, that they were in a particular and close relation to the civil government of the district in which each was planted, and that their absolute dependence upon the mother house, and their close observance of one rule, lent the whole order something of the force of an army.

The Cluniac influence came early into the Thames Valley. By the beginning of the twelfth century, and within fifty years of the Conquest, this new influence was found interpolated with and imposed upon the five centuries that had hitherto been wholly dependent upon the three great Benedictine posts. This Cluniac foundation, the first of the new houses on the Thames, was fixed upon the peninsula of Reading.

It was in 1121 that the son of the Conqueror brought the Cluniac order to the little town. From the moment of the foundation of the abbey it attracted, in part by its geographical position, in part by the fact that it was the first great new foundation upon the Thames, and in part by the accident which lent a special devotion or power to one particular house and which was in this case largely due to the discipline and character of the Cluniac order, Reading took on a very high position in England. It had about it, if one may so express oneself, something more modern, something more direct and political than was to be found in the old Benedictine houses that had preceded it. The work it had to do was less material: the fields were already drained, the life and wealth of the new civilisation had begun, and throughout the four hundred years of its existence the function of Reading was rather to entertain the Court, to assist at parliaments, and to be, throughout, the support of the monarchy. It sprang at once into this position, and its architecture symbolised to some extent the rapid command which it acquired, for it preserved to the end the characteristics of the early century in which it was erected: the Norman arch, the dog-tooth ornaments, the thick walls, the barbaric capitals of the early twelfth century.

Before the thirteenth it was in wealth equal to, and in public repute the superior of, any foundation upon the banks of the Thames with the exception of Westminster itself, and it forms, with the three Benedictine foundations, and with the later foundation of Osney, the last link in the chain of abbeys which ran unbroken from stage to stage throughout the whole length of the river. And with it ends the story of those first foundations which completed the recivilisation of the Valley.

Reading was not the only Cluniac establishment upon the Thames. Another, and earlier one, was to be found at Bermondsey; but its proximity to London and its distance down river forbid it having any place in these pages. It was founded immediately after the Conquest; Lanfranc colonised it with French monks; it became an abbacy at the very end of the fourteenth century, and was remarkable for its continual accretion of wealth, an accretion in some part due to the growing importance of London throughout its existence. At the end of the thirteenth century it stands worth £280. At the time of its dissolution, on 1 January 1538, in spite of the much higher value of money in the sixteenth century as compared with the thirteenth, it stands worth over £500: £10,000 a year.

A relic of its building remained (but only a gatehouse) till 1805.

Osney also dated from the early twelfth century, and was almost contemporary with Reading.

It stood just outside the walls of Oxford Castle to the west, and upon the bank of the main stream of the Thames, and owed its foundation to the Conqueror's local governing family of Oilei. Though at the moment of its suppression it hardly counted a fifth of the revenues of Westminster (which must be our standard throughout all this examination), yet its magnificence profoundly affected contemporaries, and has left a great tradition. It must always be remembered that these great monasteries were not only receivers of revenue as are our modern rich, but were also producers or, rather, could be producers when they chose, and that therefore the actual economic power of any one foundation might always be higher, and often was very considerably higher, than the nominal revenue, the dead income, which passed to the spoliators of the sixteenth century. When a town is sacked the army gets a considerable loot, but nothing like what the value was of the city as it flourished before the siege.

At any rate, whether Osney owed its magnificence to internal industry, to a wise expenditure, or to a severity of life which left a large surplus for ornament and extension, it was for 400 years the principal building upon the upper river, catching the eye from miles away up by Eynsham meadows and forming a noble gate to the University town for those who approached it from the west by the packway, of which traces still remain, and over the bridges which the Conqueror had built. So deep was the impress of Osney upon the locality, and even upon the national Government, that Henry proposed, as in the case of Westminster, to make of the building one of his new cathedrals, and to establish there his new See of Oxford. The determination, however, lasted but for a very short time. In a few years the financial pressure was too much for him; he transferred the see to the old Church of St Frideswides, where it still remains, and gave up Osney to loot. It was looted very thoroughly.

The smaller monasteries need hardly a mention. At the head of them comes Eynsham, worth more than half as much as Osney, and a very considerable place. Founded as a colony or adjunct to Stow, in Lincolnshire, it outlived the importance of the parent house, and was at the height of its prosperity immediately before the Dissolution.

Eynsham affords a very good instance of the way in which the fabric in these superb temples disappeared. As late as the early eighteenth century there was still standing the whole of the west front; the two high towers, the splendid west window, and the sculptured doorways were complete, though they remained but as a fragment of a ruined building. A century and a half passed and the whole had disappeared, carted away to build walls and stables for the local squires, or sold by the local squires for rubble.

Of the little priory at Lechlade very little is known, save that it was founded in the thirteenth century and had disappeared long before the Reformation, while of that at Cricklade we know even less, save that it humbly survived and was counted in the 'bag' at only four pounds a year.

With Dorchester, which had existed from the twelfth century, and which was worth almost half as much as Eynsham, and with the considerable Cell of Hurley which attached to Westminster, the list is complete. It is interesting to know that the church at Dorchester was saved by the local patriotism of one man, who left half his fortune for the purchase of it, and that not in order to ruin it and to sell the stones of it, but in order to preserve it: a singular man.

In a general survey of monastic influence in the Valley of the Thames, it would be natural to omit the foundations which belonged to the later Middle Ages. It was in the Dark Ages that the great Benedictine work was done, the pastures drained, the woods planted, the settlements established. It was in the early Middle Ages, in the twelfth and thirteenth centuries and in the first half of the fourteenth – in a word, before the Black Death – that the work of the new and vigorous foundations, and the revived energy of the older ones, spread Gothic architecture, scholastic learning, and the whole reinvigorated social system of the time, from Oxford to Westminster; and the historian who notes

the social and economic effects of monasticism in Western
Europe, however enthusiastic he may be in defence of that
force, cannot with truth lend it between the Black Death
and the Reformation a vigour which it did not possess. It
had tended to become, in the fifteenth century, a fixed
social institution like any other, one might almost say a
bundle of proprietary rights like any other. And though it
is easy now to perceive what ruin was caused by the sudden
destruction, the contemporaries of the last age of Great
Houses were perpetually considering their privilege and
their immovable tradition rather than the remaining functions which the monasteries fulfilled in the State.

On this account historical notes dealing with the development of the Thames Valley would naturally omit a refer-
ence to foundations existing only from the close of the
Middle Ages. But an exception must be made to this rule in
the case of Sheen.

Sheen was a Charterhouse, and it merits observation
not only from the peculiar characteristics of the Carthusian Order, but also from its considerable position so near
to Westminster and not yet overshadowed by the greatness
either of that abbey or of Chertsey. It received, from its
land in England alone, a revenue of close upon two-thirds
of that which Westminster enjoyed. Recent in its origin (it
had existed for only just over 100 years when Henry VIII
attacked it), not without that foreign flavour which, rightly
or wrongly, was ascribed in this island to the Carthusian
Order, rigid in doctrine, and of a magnificent temper in the
defence of religion, these Carthusians, like their brethren in
London, formed a very natural target for the King's attack.

I include them only because notes upon the mediæval foundations, would be quite imperfect were there no mention of Sheen, late as the origin of the community was, and little as it had to do with the historic development of the valley.

This completes the list of the greater foundations; with the lesser ones it would only be possible to deal in pages devoted to the Monastic Institution alone. The very numerous communities of friars, and the hospitals in the towns upon the Thames, cannot be mentioned, the little nunneries of Ankerwick, Burnham, and Little Marlow, the communities, early and late, of Medmenham and Cholsey, the priories of Lechlade and of Cricklade (which might have occupied a larger space than was available), must be passed over. Even Godstow, famous as it is from the early legend of Rosamond, and considerable as was its function both of education and of retreat, cannot be included in the list of those principal foundations which alone take rank as originators of the prosperity of the valley.

Several of these smaller houses went in the Dissolution to swell the revenues of Bisham, the new community which Henry, as he said, intended to take the place of much that he had destroyed; and Bisham would be very well worth a considerable attention from the reader had it survived. But it did not survive. Hardly was it founded when Henry himself immediately destroyed it, and, as we shall see later, Bisham affords one of the most curious and instructive examples of the way in which that large monastic revenue, which it was certainly intended to keep in the hands of the Crown, and which, had it been so kept, would have given to England the strongest Central Government in Europe, drifted into the hands of the squires, multiplied perhaps by ten the wealth of their class, and transformed the Government of England into that oligarchy which was completed in the seventeenth century, and which, though permeated and transformed by Jewish finance, is standing in a precarious strength to this day.

Westminster, Chertsey, Sheen, Reading, Abingdon, and Osney disappeared.

One writes the list straight off without considering, taking it for granted that everything which could have roused the cupidity of that generation necessarily disappeared: and as one writes it one remembers that, after all, Westminster survived. Its survival was an accident, which will be further considered. But that survival, so far from redeeming, emphasises and throws into relief the destruction of the rest.

Of these enduring monuments of human energy and, what is more important still in the control of energy, human certitude, what besides Westminster survived? Of Chertsey there is perhaps a gateway and part of a wall; of Sheen nothing; of Reading a few flints built into modern work; of Abingdon a gateway, and a buttress or two that long served to support a brewhouse; of Osney nothing, contrariwise, electric works and the slums of a modern town. All these were Westminsters. In all of these was to be discovered that patient process of production which argues the continuity, and therefore the dignity, of human civilisation. Each had the glass which we can no longer paint, the vivid, living, and happy grotesque in sculpture which only the best of us can so much as understand; each had a thousand and another thousand details of careful work in stone meant to endure, if not for ever, at least into such further centuries as might have the added faith and added knowledge to restore them in greater plenitude. The whole thing has gone. It has gone to no purpose. Nothing has been built upon it save a wandering host of rich and careworn men.

Suppose a man to have gone down the Thames when the new discussions were beginning in London and (as was customary even at the close of the Middle Ages) were spreading from town to town with a rapidity that we, who have ceased to debate ideas, can never understand. Let such a traveller or bargeman have gone down from Cricklade to the Tower, how would the Great Houses have appeared to him?

The upper river would have been much the same, but as he came to that part of it which was wealthy and populous, as he turned the corner of Witham Hill, he would already have seen far off, larger and a little nearer than the many spires of Oxford, a building such as to-day we never see save in our rare and half-deserted cathedral country towns. It was the Abbey of Osney. It would have been his land-mark, as Hereford is the landmark for a man to-day rowing up to Wye, or the new spire of Chichester for a man that makes harbour out of the channel past Bisham upon a rising tide. And as he passed beneath it (for, of the many branches here, the main stream took him that way) he would have seen a great and populous place with nothing ruinous in it, all well ordered, busy with men and splendid; here again that which we now look upon as a relic and a circumstance of repose was once alive and strong.

Upon his way beneath the old stone bridge which crossed the ford, and shooting between the lifted paddles of the weirs, he would, once below Oxford, have seen much the same pastures that we see to-day; but in a few hours Abingdon, the next to Osney, would have fixed his eyes as Osney had before.

Abingdon would have been to him what Noyon is on the Oise, or any of our river cathedrals in Western Europe – an apse pointing up stream, though rounded and lacking the flying buttresses of the Gothic, for it was thick, broad, and Norman. Here also, as one may believe, from its situation, trees would have shrouded somewhat what he saw. There are few such riverside apses in Christian Europe that are not screened in this manner by trees planted between the stream and them. But as he drifted farther down, before he reached the bridge, the west front would have burst upon him, quite new, exceedingly rich and proud, a strict example, one may believe, of the Perpendicular, and of what was for the first time, and for a moment only, a true English Gothic. It would have stood out before him, catching the sun of the afternoon in its maze of glass. It would have seemed a thing to endure; within his lifetime it was to be utterly destroyed.

Once more in the many reaches between Abingdon and Wallingford, the sights would have been those which a man sees now. And though at Wallingford he would have had before him a town of brilliant red tiles and timberwork, and a town perhaps larger than that which we see to-day, yet (could such a man come to life again) the contrast would not strike him here, and still less in the fields below, so much as when he came near to Reading.

That everything else of age in Reading has disappeared one need not say, but were that traveller here to-day, the thing that he would most seek for and most lack would be the bulk of the building at the farther end of the town.

One can best say what it was by saying that it was like Durham. It is true that Durham Cathedral stands upon a noble cliff overhanging a ravine, while Reading Abbey stood upon a small and irregular hill which hardly showed above the flat plains of the river meadows, but in massiveness of structure and in type of architecture Reading seems to have resembled Durham more nearly than any other of our great monuments, and to emphasise its parallelism to Durham is perhaps the best way to make the modern reader understand what we have lost.

Nothing that he had seen in this journey would more have sunk into the mind of a contemporary man, nothing that he would lack were he resuscitated to-day would leave a want more grievous. In the destruction of Reading the people of this country lost something which not even their aptitude for foreign travel can replace.

Windsor, as he passed, stood up above the right of him, not very different from what we still admire as we come down from Bray and look up to the jutting fore-tower which is worthy of Coucy. But down below Windsor (after whose bridge we to-day see nothing whatever of value), just after he had passed the wooden bridge of Staines and shot the weir of that town, the river bent southward.

The traveller would have found Pentonhook already forming or formed, and when he had got round it he would have seen soaring above him down stream the great mass of Chertsey Abbey. If Reading had the solidity and the barbaric grandeur of Durham, Chertsey had in an ecclesiastical way the vastness of Windsor, and must have seemed like a town to anyone approaching it thus down the river. The enclosed area of the abbey buildings alone covered four acres.

This impression which such a traveller would have received of the great religious houses was enhanced by something more than the magnitude and splendour of the buildings. Divided as was opinion at that moment upon their value to the State, and jealous as had become land-less men of the long traditions and privileges of the monks, these still represented not only their own wealth but the general accumulation of capital and the continued prosperity of the river valley. It is true to say, in spite of the difficulty of appreciating such a truth in the light of our knowledge of what was to follow, that the destruction of such foundations would have seemed to the traveller before the Dissolution inconceivable. Nevertheless it came.

These notes are not the place in which to discuss that most difficult of all historical problems – I mean the causes which led the nation to abandon in a couple of generations the whole of its traditions and to adopt, not spontaneously but at the bidding of a comparatively small body of wealthy men, a new scheme of society. But it is of value to consider the economic aspect of the thing, and to show what it was that Henry desired to seize when his policy of Dissolution was secretly formed.

The economic function of the monastic system in the Middle Ages, and especially in the later Middle Ages, is one to which no sufficient attention has been given by historians.

They collected, as does no modern agency, wealth from very various sources, scattered up and down the whole of the kingdom, and often farther afield, throughout Europe, and exercised the whole economic power so drawn together in one centre, and so founded a permanent nucleus of wealth in the place where the community resided.

We are indeed to-day accustomed to a similar effect in the action of our wealthy families. The rents of the London poor, a toll upon the produce of Egypt, of the Argentine, or of India, all flow into some country house in the provinces, where it revives in an effective demand for production, or lends to the whole countryside a wealth which, of itself, it could never have produced. The neighbourhood of Aylesbury, the palaces of the larger territorials, are modern examples of this truth, that the economic power of a district does not reside in its productive capacity, but in its capacity for effective demand. And it is undoubtedly true that if there were anything permanent in modern society we should be witnessing in the wealthier quarters of Paris and London, in the Riviera in the holiday part of Egypt, and in certain centres of provincial luxury in England, in France, and in Western Germany, the foundation of a permanent economic superiority.

But nothing in modern society has any roots. Where to-day is some one of these great territorial houses in fifty years there may be nothing but decay. Fashion may change from the Riviera to some other part of the Mediterranean littoral, and with fashion will go the concentration of wealth which accompanies it.

In the Middle, and especially in the latter Middle, Ages it was otherwise. The great religious houses not only tended to accumulate wealth and to perpetuate it in the same hands (they could not gamble it away nor disperse it in luxury; they could hardly waste it by mismanagement), but they were also permanently fixed on one spot.

Such an institution as Reading, for example, or as Abingdon, went on perpetually receiving its immense revenues for generation after generation, and were under no temptation or rather had no capacity for spending it elsewhere than in the situation where their actual buildings were to be found.

In this way the great monastic houses founded a tradition of local wealth which has profoundly affected the history of the Thames Valley. And if that valley is still to-day one of the chief districts wherein the economic power of England is concentrated, it owes that position mainly to the centuries during which the great foundations exercised their power upon the banks of the river.

The growth of great towns, one of the last phases of our national development, one which finds its example in the Thames Valley as elsewhere, and one to which we shall allude before closing these notes upon the river, has somewhat obscured the quality of this original accumulation of wealth along the Thames. But when we come to consider the figures of the census at an earlier time, before modern commercialism and the railway had drawn wealth and population into fewer and larger centres, we shall see how considerable was the string of towns which had grown up along the stream. And we shall especially see how fairly divided among them was the population, and, it may be presumed, the wealth and the rateable value, of the valley.

The point just mentioned in connection with the larger monastic foundations, and their artificial concentration of economic power, deserves a further elaboration, for the economic importance of a district is one of the aspects of geography which even modern analysis has dealt with very imperfectly.

Economists speak of the economic importance of such-and-such a spot because material of use to man-kind is there discovered. Thus, people commonly point to the economic importance of the valleys all round the Pennine Range in England because they contain coal and metals, and to the economic importance of a small district in South Wales for the same reason.

A further consideration has admitted that not only places where things useful to mankind are discovered, but places naturally fitted for their exchange have an economic importance peculiarly their own. Indeed, the more history is studied from the point of view of economics, the more does this kind of natural opportunity emerge, and the less does the political importance of purely productive areas appear. The mountain districts of Spain, the Cornish peninsula, were centres of metallic industry of the first importance to the Romans, but they remained poor throughout the period of Roman civilisation. To-day the farmer in the west of America, the miner and the clerk in Johannesburg, are perhaps more numerous, but as a political force no wealthier for the opportunities of their sites: the economic power which they ultimately produce is first concentrated in the centres of exchange where the wealth they produce is handled.

Now there is a third basis for the economic importance of a district, and as this third basis is indefinitely more important than the other two, it has naturally been overlooked in the analysis of the universities. This basis is the basis of residence. Given that a conqueror, or a seat of Government established by routine, is established in a particular place and chooses there to remain; or given that the pleasure attached to a particular site – its natural pleasures or the inherited grandeur of its buildings or what not – make it an established residence for those who control the expenditure of wealth, then that place will acquire an economic importance which has for its foundation nothing more material than the human will. Thither wealth, wherever produced, will flow, and there will be discovered that ultimate motive force of all production and of all exchange, the effective demand of those possessors who alone can set the industrial machine in motion.

This has been abundantly true in every period of the world's history, whenever commerce existed upon a considerable scale, or whenever a military force sufficiently universal was at the command of wealthy men.

It is particularly true to-day. To-day not the natural centres of exchange, still less the natural centres of production, determine what places in the world shall be wealthy and what shall not. The surplus of the wealth produced by the Egyptian fellaheen is carefully collected by English officials and largely consumed in Paris; the wealth produced by the manufacturers of North England is largely spent in the south of England and upon the Continent; until their recent and successful revolt, the wealth produced by the Irish peasantry was largely spent in London and upon the Riviera.

The economic importance, then, of the Thames Valley has not diminished, but increased since South England ceased to be the main field of production.

The tradition of Government, the habitual residence of the wealthy and directing classes of the community, have centred more and more in London. The old establishment of luxury in the Thames Valley has perpetually increased since the decline of its industrial and agricultural importance, and undoubtedly, if it were possible to draw a map indicating the proportion of economic *demand* throughout the country, the Valley of the Thames would appear, in proportion to its population, by far the most concentrated district in England, although it contains but one very large town, and although it is innocent of any very important modern industry.

It is interesting, in connection with this economic aspect of the Thames Valley, to note that, alone of the great river valleys of Europe, it has no railway system parallel to its banks. There is no series of productive centres which could give rise to such a railway system. The Great Western Railway follows the river now some distance upon one side, now some distance upon the other, as far as Oxford; but it does not depend in any way upon the stream, and where the course of the stream is irregular it goes on its straight course, throwing out branch lines to the smaller towns upon the banks: for the railway depends, so far as this section is concerned, upon the industries of the Midlands and of the west. Were you to cut off the sources of carriage which it draws upon from beyond the Valley of the Thames it could not exist.

The Scheldt, the Rhine, the Rhône, the Garonne, the Seine, the Elbe, are all different in this from the Thames. The economic power of our main river valley is chiefly a spending power. It produces little and, though it exchanges more of human wealth, it is the artificial machinery of exchange rather than the physical movement of goods that enriches it.

Now this habit of residence, this settlement of the concentrated power of demand upon the banks of the Thames, was the work of the monastic houses. It may be argued that, with the commercial importance of London, and with its attainment of the position of a capital, the residence of such economic power would necessarily have spread up the Thames Valley. It is doubtful whether any such necessity as this existed. In Roman times the Thames certainly did not lead up thus in the line of wealth from London, and though it is true that water carriage greatly increased in importance after the breakdown of Roman civilisation, yet the medium by which that water carriage was utilised was the medium of the Benedictine foundations. They it was who established that continuous line of progressive agricultural development and who prepared the way for the later yet more continuous line of the full monastic effort which succeeded the Conquest.

A list of monastic institutions upon the river, if we exclude the friars, the hospitals, and such foundations as made part of town or university life, is as follows: – a priory at Cricklade, another at Lechlade, the Abbey at Eynsham (sufficiently near the stream to be regarded as riparian), the Nunnery and School of Godstow, the great Abbeys of Osney and Rewley, the Benedictine Nunnery at Littlemore, the great Abbey of Abingdon, the Abbey of Dorchester, Cholsey (but this had been destroyed before the Conquest, and was never revived), the Augustinian Nunnery at Goring, the great Cluniac Abbey at Reading, the Cell of Westminster at Hurley, the Abbey of Medmenham, the Abbey of Bisham just opposite Marlow, and the Nunnery of Little Marlow; the Nunnery of Burnham, which, though nearly a mile and a half from the stream, should count from the position of its property as a riparian foundation, the little Nunnery of Ankerwike, the great Benedictine Abbey of Chertsey, the Carthusians of Sheen, and the Benedictines of Westminster, to which may be added the foundation of Bermondsey.

When the end came the total number of those in control of such wide possessions was small.

Indeed it was perhaps no small cause of the unpopularity, such as it was, into which the same monasteries had locally fallen, that so much economic power was concentrated in so few hands. The greater foundations throughout the country possessed but a little more than 3000 religious, and even when all the nuns, friars, and professed religious of the towns are counted, we do not arrive at more than 8000 in religion in an England which must have had a population of at least 4 million, and quite possibly a much larger number; nor could the mobs foresee that the class which would seize upon the abbey lands would concentrate the means of production into still fewer hands, until at last the mass of Englishmen should have no lot in England.

Moreover, it would be an error to consider the numbers of the religious alone. The smaller foundations, and especially the convents of nuns, did certainly support but small numbers, and this probably accounts for the ease with which they were suppressed, but, on the other hand, their possessions also were small. In the case of the great foundations, though one can count but 3000 monks and canons, the number of them must be multiplied many times if we are to arrive at the total of the communities concerned. Reading, Abingdon, and the rest were little cities, with a whole population of direct dependants living within the walls, and a still larger number of families without, who indirectly depended upon the revenues of the abbey for their livelihood.

Another and perhaps a better way of presenting to a modern reader the overwhelming economic power of the mediæval monastic system, especially its economic power in the Valley of the Thames, would be to add to such a list of houses a map of that valley showing the manors in ecclesiastical hands, the freeholds and leaseholds held by the great abbeys, in addition to the livings that were within their gift; in a word, a map giving all their different forms of revenue.

Such a map would show the Valley of the Thames and its tributaries covered with ecclesiastical influence upon every side.

Even if we confined ourselves to the parishes upon the actual banks of the river, the map would present a continuous stretch of possessions upon either side from far above Eynsham down to below bridges.

The research that would be necessary for the establishment of such a complete list would require a leisure which is not at the disposal of the present writer, but it is possible to give some conception of what the monastic holdings were by drawing up a list confined to but a small part of these holdings and showing therefore *a fortiori* what the total must have been.

In this list I concern myself only with the eight largest houses in the whole length of the river. I do not mention parishes from which the revenues were not important (though these were numerous, for the abbeys held a large number of small parcels of land). I do not mention the very numerous holdings close to the river but not actually upon it (such as Burnham or Watereaton), nor, which is most important of all, do I count even in the riparian holdings such foundations as were not themselves set upon the banks of the Thames. Whatever Thames land paid rent to a monastery not actually situated upon the banks of the river, I omit. Finally the list, curtailed as it is by all these limitations, concerns only the land held at the moment of the Dissolution. Scores of holdings, such as those of Lechlade, which was dissolved in Catholic times, Windsor, which was exchanged as we have seen at the time of the Conquest, I omit and confine myself only to the lands held at the time of the Dissolution.

Yet these lands – though they concern only eight monasteries, though I mention only those actually upon the banks of the river, and though I omit from the list all small payments – put before one a series of names which, to those familiar with the Thames, seems almost like a voyage along the stream and appears to cover every portion of the landscape with which travellers upon the river are familiar. Thus we have Shifford, Eynsham, South Stoke, Radley, Cumnor, Witham, Botley, the Hinkseys, Sandford, Shillingford, Swinford, Medmenham, Appleford, Sutton, Wittenham, Culham, Abingdon, Goring, Cowley, Littlemore, Cholsey, Nuneham, Wallingford, Pangbourne, Streatley, Stanton Harcourt; and all this crowd of names upon the upper river is arrived at without counting such properties as attached to the great monasteries within towns, as, for example, to the monasteries of Oxford. It is true that not all these names represent complete manorial ownership. In a number of cases they stand for portions of the manor only, but even in this list ten at least, and possibly twelve, stand for complete manorial ownership. Then one must add Sonning, Wargreave, Tilehurst, Chertsey, Egham, Cobham, Richmond, Ham, Mortlake, Sheen, Kew, Chiswick, Staines, etc., of which many of the most important, such as Staines, are full manorial possessions.

It is clearly evident, from such a very imperfect and rapidly drawn list, what was the economic power of the great houses, and one may conclude, even from the basis of such imperfect evidence, that the directing force of economic effort throughout the Thames Valley was to be found, right up to the Dissolution, in the chapter houses of Reading, of Chertsey, and of Westminster, of Abingdon and of the lesser houses.

In a word, the business of Henry might be compared

to what may be in future the business of some democratic European Government when it lays its hands upon the fortunes of the great financial houses, but with this double difference, that the confiscation to which Henry bent himself was a confiscation of capital whose product did not leave the country, and could not be used for anti-national purposes, as also that it was the confiscation of wealth which never acted secretly and which had no interest, as have our chief moneylenders, in political corruption. It was a vast undertaking and, in the truest sense of the word, a revolutionary one, such as Europe had not seen until that moment, and perhaps has not seen since.

It was effected with ease, because there did not reside in the public opinion of the time any strong body of resistance.

The change of religion, in so far as a change was threatened (and upon that the mass of the parish priests themselves, and still more the mass of the laity, were very hazy), did not affect the mind of a people famous throughout Europe for their intense and often superstitious devotion; but in some odd way the segregation of the great communities, their vast wealth, and perhaps an external contradiction between their original office and their present privilege, forbade any united or widespread enthusiasm in their defence.

Englishmen rose upon every side when they thought that the vital mysteries of the Faith were threatened. The risings were only put down by the use of foreign mercenaries and by the most execrable cruelty, nor would even these means have sufficed had the rebels formed a clear plan, or had the purpose of Henry himself in matters of religion been definite and capable of definite attack. But the country, though ready to fight for Dogma, was not ready to fight for the monasteries. It might, perhaps, have fought if the attack upon them had been direct and universal. If Henry had laid down a programme of suppressing religious bodies in general, he probably could not have carried it out, but he laid down no such programme. The Dissolution of the smaller houses was imagined by the most devout to be a statesmanlike measure. Many of them, like Medmenham, were decayed; their wealth was not to be used for the private luxury of the King or of nobles; it was to swell the revenues of the greater foundations or to be applied to pious or honourable public use. But the example once given, the attack upon the greater houses necessarily followed; and the whole episode is a vivid lesson in the capital principle of statesmanship that men are governed by routine and by the example of familiar things. Render possible to the mass of men the conception that the road they habitually follow is not a necessity of their lives, and you may exact of them almost any sacrifice or hope to see them witness without disgust almost any enormity.

Moreover, the great monasteries were each severally tricked. The one was asked to surrender at one time, another at another; the one for this reason, the other for that. The suppression of Chertsey, the example perpetually recurring in these pages, was solemnly promised to be but a transference of the community from one spot to another; then when the transference had taken place the second community was ruthlessly destroyed. There is ample evidence to show that each community had its special hope of survival, and that each, until quite the end of the process, regarded its fate, when that fate fell upon it, as something exceptional and peculiar to itself. Some, or rather many, purchased temporary exemption, doubtless secure in the belief that their bribe would make that extension permanent. Their payments were accepted, but the contracts depending upon them were never fulfilled.

When the Dissolution had taken place, apart from the private loot, which was enormous, and to which we shall turn a few pages hence, a methodical destruction took place on the part of the Crown.

In none of the careless waste which marked the time is there a worse example than in the case of Reading. The lead had already been stripped from the roof and melted into pigs; the timbers of the roof had already been rotting for nearly thirty years, when Elizabeth gave leave for such of them as were sound to be removed. Some were used in the repairing of a local church; a little later further leave was given for 200 cartloads of freestone to be removed from the ruins. But they showed an astonishing tenacity. The abbey was still a habitation before the Civil Wars, and even at the end of the eighteenth century a very considerable stretch of the old walls remained.

Westminster was saved.

The salvation of Westminster is the more remarkable in that the house was extremely wealthy.

Upon nothing has more ink been wasted in the minute research of modern history than upon an attempted exact comparison between modern and mediæval economics.

It is a misfortune that those who are best fitted to appreciate the economic problems and science of the modern world are, either by race or religion, or both, cut off from the mediæval system, and even when they are acquainted with the skeleton, as it were, of that body of Christian Europe, are none the less out of sympathy with, or even ignorant of, its living form and spirit.

The particular department of that inquiry which concerns anyone who touches the vast economic revolution produced by the Dissolution of the monasteries is the comparison of values (as measured in the precious metals) between the early sixteenth century and the early twentieth.

No sensible man needs to be told that such a comparison is one of the very numerous parts of historical inquiry in which a better result is arrived at in proportion as the matter is more generally and largely observed. It is one in which detail is more fatal to a man even than inaccuracy, and it is one in which hardly a single observer who has been really soaked in his subject has avoided the most ludicrous conclusions.

Again, no man of common sense need be told that a rigid multiple is absolutely impossible of discovery. The search for such a multiple is like a search for an index number which shall apply to all the varying economic habits of the modern world. One cannot say: 'Multiply prices by 10' or 'Multiply prices by 20', and thus afford the modern reader a sound basis; but one can say, after some observation: 'Multiply by such-and-such a multiple' (wherever very large and varied expenditure is concerned) and you will certainly have a minimum; though how much *more* such expenditure may have represented in those very different and far simpler social circumstances cannot be precisely determined.

What, then, is the rough multiple that will give us our minimum?

The inquiry has been prosecuted by more than one authority upon the basis of wheat. One may say that wheat in normal years in the early sixteenth century stood at about an eighth of wheat in what I may call the normal years of the nineteenth, before the influx of Colonial produce began to be serious, and before the depreciation of silver combined with other causes to disturb prices.

Those who have taken wheat for their basis, recognising, as even they must do, that 8 is far too low a multiple, are willing to grant 10, and sometimes even 12, and this way of calculating, largely because it is a ready rule, has entered into many books upon the Reformation. The early Tudor penny is turned into the modern shilling.

But this basis of calculation is false, because the eating of wheaten bread was not then the universal thing it is to-day. The English proletarian of to-day is, in comparison with the large well-to-do class of his fellow-citizens, a far poorer man than his ancestry ever were. Wheaten bread is, indeed, his necessity, but good fresh meat (for example) is an exception for him.

Now the Englishmen of earlier times made beef a necessity, and yet we find that beef will permit a higher multiple than wheat. Beef will give you a multiple of 12, and just as wheat, giving you a multiple of 8, permits a somewhat higher general multiple, so beef, giving you a multiple of 12, permits a higher one. So if we were to make beef our staple instead of wheat we should get a multiple of 13 or 14 by which to turn the money of the first third of the sixteenth century into the money of our own time.

But beef, in its turn, is not a fair standard; during much of the year pork had, under the circumstances of the time, to be eaten instead of fresh meat. Pork is to-day almost the only meat all the year round of many labourers on the land. Now pork gives a still higher multiple: it gives 20. For the pound that you would now give in Chichester Market for a breeding sow, you gave in the early years of the sixteenth century a shilling. So here you have another article of common consumption which gives you a multiple of 20.

Strong ale gives you a higher multiple still – one of nearly 24. You could then get strong ale at a penny a gallon. You will hardly get it at two shillings a gallon to-day; and yet it is made of the same materials. The small ale of the hayfield will give you almost any multiple you like; it is from eight-pence to ninepence a gallon now: it was often given away in the sixteenth century as water would be.

The consideration of but a few sets of prices such as those we have quoted shows that the ordinary multiple might be anything between 8 and 24, with a prejudice in favour of the higher rather than the lower figure. But there are other lines of proof which converge upon the matter, and which permit a greater degree of certitude. For instance, even after the rise in prices in the early part of Elizabeth's reign, while sixpence a week is thought low for the board and lodging of a working man, a shilling is thought very high, and is only given in the case of first-rate artisans; and if we consider the pre-Reformation period, when the position of the labourer was, of course, much better than it was under Elizabeth, or ever has been since, we find something of the same scale. A penny a day is thought a rather mean allowance, but twopence a day is a first-rate extra board wage.

Again, in Henry VIII's first poll tax it is taken for granted that many labourers have less than a pound a year in actual wages, and that wages over this sum, up to two pounds, for instance, form a sort of aristocracy of labour that can afford to pay taxation. Of course some part of the wages so counted were paid in part board and lodging, especially in the agricultural industries, but still, the reception of 240 pence for a year's work in money gives you a multiple of far more than 20: you will not get a man about a house and garden for less than thirty pounds though you feed and house him, and the unhoused outside labourer gets, first and last, over fifty pounds at the least.

When the Reformation was in full swing the currency was debased almost out of recognition, and before the death of Edward VI prices are rendered so fictitious by inflation that they are useless for our purpose. It is only with the currency of Elizabeth that they became true measures of value once more.

It is useless, therefore, to follow the inquiry after the Dissolution of the monasteries, for not only was the currency at sixes and sevens, but true prices were also rapidly rising with the influx of precious metals from Spain and America.

I have said enough in this very elementary sketch to show that a general multiple of 20, when one considers wages as well as staple foods, is as high as can be fixed safely, while a general multiple of 12 is certainly too low.

But even to multiply by 20 is by no means enough if one is to appreciate the social meaning of such-and-such a large income in the first part of Henry VIII's reign.

A brief historical essay, such as is this, is no place in which to discuss any general theory of economics; were there space to do so, even in an elementary fashion, it would be possible to show how the increase of wealth in a state is, on account of the increased elasticity in circulation of the currency, almost independent of the movement of prices. But without going into formulæ; of this complexity, a couple of homely comparisons will suffice to show what a much larger thing a given income was in the early sixteenth century, than its corresponding amount in values is to-day.

Consider a man with some £2000 a year travelling through modern Europe. Prices, in the competition of modern commerce and the ease of modern travel, are levelled up very evenly throughout the area that he traverses. Yet such a man, should he settle in a village of Spanish peasants, would appear of almost illimitable wealth, because he would have at his command an almost indefinite amount of those simple necessities which form the whole category of their consumable values. Or again, let such a man settle in a place where the variety of consumable values is large, but where the distribution of wealth is fairly equal, and the small income, therefore, a normal social phenomenon – as, for instance, among the lower middle class of Paris – there again his £2000 a year would be of much greater effect than in a society where wealth was unequally divided, for

it would produce that effect in a medium where the satis-
faction of nearly every individual around him was easily
reached upon perhaps a tenth of such an income.

When all this is taken into consideration we can begin
to see what the great monasteries were at the time of their
dissolution. It is hardly an exaggeration to multiply the list
of mere values by 20 to bring it into the terms of modern
currency. A place worth close on £2000 a year (as was, for
instance, Ramsey Abbey) meant an income of not far short
of £40,000 a year in our money, to go by prices alone. And
that £40,000 a year was spent in an England in which nine-
tenths of the luxury of our modern rich was unknown, in
which the squire was usually but three or four times richer
than one of his farmers, in which great wealth, where it
existed, attached rather to an office than to a person. In
general, the multiple of 20 must be further multiplied by
a coefficient which is not arithmetically determinable, but
which we see to be very large by a general comparison of
the small, poor, and equable society of the early sixteenth
century with the complex, huge, wealthy, and wholly iniq-
uitous society of our own day.

Supposing, for instance, we take the high multiple of 20,
and say that the revenues of Westminster at its dissolution
in the first days of 1540 were some £80,000 a year in our
modern money, we are far underestimating the economic
position of Westminster in the State. There are to-day
many private men in London who dispose of as great an
income, and who, for all their ostentation, are not remarkable; but the income of Westminster in the early sixteenth
century, when wealth was far more equally divided than it

is now, and when the accumulation of it was far less, was a very different matter to what we mean to-day by £80,000 a year. It produced more of the effect which we might to-day imagine would be produced by a million. The fortune of but very few families could so much as compare with it, and the fortunes of individual families, especially of wealthy families, were, during the existence of a strong king, highly perilous, and often cut short; nothing could pretend to equal such an economic power but the Crown, which then was, and which remained until the victory of the aristocracy in the Civil Wars, by far the richest legal personality in Britain. The temptation to sack Westminster was something like the temptation presented to our financial powers to-day to get at the rubber of the Congo Basin or at the unexploited coal of Northern China.

By a miracle that temptation was withstood. For the moment Henry intended to construct a bishopric with its cathedral out of the old corporation and abbey. He might have done so and yet have yielded immediately after to his cupidity, as he did with the Cathedral of Osney. It ended in the form which it at present maintains. The greater part of its revenues were, of course, stolen, but the fabric was spared and enough income was retained to permit the continuous life of Westminster to our own time.

Men are slow to conceive what might have been – nay, what almost *was* – in their national history; it seems difficult to our generation to imagine Westminster Abbey absent only from the national life; yet Abingdon is gone, all but a gateway, Reading all but a few ruined walls, Chertsey has utterly disappeared, so has Osney, so has Sheen

– to mention the great river houses alone: Westminster alone survives, and the only reason it survives is that it had about it at the time of the destruction of the monasteries a royal flavour, and that its existence helped to bolster up the Tudors. But for that it would have been sold like the rest, the lead would have been stripped from its roof, the glass broken and thrown aside, and a Cecil or a Howard would have built himself a palace with the stones. It is but a chance that the words 'Westminster Abbey' mean more to us to-day than 'Woburn Abbey', 'Bewley Abbey' or any one of the scores of 'Abbeys', 'Priories', and the rest, which are the names of our country houses.

Chertsey and Abingdon were less fortunate than Westminster.

Chertsey, indeed, has so thoroughly disappeared that it might be taken as a symbol of all that England had been for the thirty generations since Christianity had come to her, and then, in two generations of men, ceased suddenly to be. There is, perhaps, not one in a thousand of the vague Colonials who regard Westminster Abbey as a sort of inevitable centre for Britishers and Anglo-Saxons, who has so much as heard of Chertsey. There is perhaps but one in a hundred of historical students who could attach a definite connection to the name, and yet Chertsey came next in the list of the great Benedictine Abbeys; Chertsey also was coeval with England.

Chertsey went the way of them all. The last abbot, John Cordery, surrendered it in the July of 1537, but he and his community were not immediately dispersed, they were taken off to fill that strange new foundation of Bisham, of which we shall hear later in connection with the river, and which in its turn immediately disappeared. Not a year had passed, the June of 1538 was not over, when the new community at Bisham was scattered as the old one at Chertsey had been.

Of the abbey itself nothing is left but a broken piece of gateway, and the few stones of a wall. But a relic of it remains in Black Cherry Fair, a market granted to the abbey in the fifteenth century and formerly held upon St Anne's Hill and upon St Anne's Day.

The fate of this monastery has something about it particularly tragic, for the abbot and the monks of Chertsey when they surrendered did so in the full expectation of continuing their monastic life at Bisham, and if Bisham was treacherously destroyed immediately after the fault does not lie at their door.

With Abingdon it was otherwise. The last prior was perhaps the least steadfast of all the many bewildered or avaricious characters that meet us in the story of the Dissolution. He was one Thomas Rowland, who had watched every movement of Henry's mind, and had, if possible, gone before. He did not even wait until the demand was made to him, but suggested the abandonment of the trust which so many generations of Englishmen had left in his hands, and he had a reward in the gift not only of a very large pension but also of the Manor of Cumnor, which had been before the destruction of the religious orders the sanatorium or country house of the monks. He obtained it: and from his time on Cumnor has borne an air of desolation and of murder, nor does any part of his own palace remain.

When any organised economic system disappears, there is nothing more interesting in history than to watch the process of its replacement: for example, the gradual disappearance of pagan slavery, and its replacement by the self-governing peasantry of the Middle Ages, with all the consequence of that change, affords some of the best reading in Continental records. But the Dissolution of the English monasteries has this added interest, that it was an immediate, and therefore an overwhelming, change; there was hardly a warning, there was no delay. Suddenly, not within the lifetime of a man, but within that of a Parliament, from one year to another, a good quarter of the whole economic power of the nation was utterly transformed. Nothing like it has been known in European history.

What filled the void so made? The answer to this question is, the Oligarchy: the landed class which had been threatening for so long to assume the Government of England stepped into the shoes of the great houses, and by this addition to their already considerable power achieved the destruction of the monarchy and within 100 years proceeded to the ordering of the English people under a small group of wealthy men, a form of Government which to this day England alone of all Christian nations suffers or enjoys.

This general statement must not be taken to mean that the oligarchic system, whose basis lies in the ownership of land, was immediately created by the Dissolution of the great monasteries. The development of the territorial system of England, of which system the banks of the Thames afford as good a picture as any in England, can be traced certainly from Saxon, and conjecturally from Roman, times.

The Roman estate was, presumably, the direct ancestor of the manor, and the Saxon thegns were perhaps most of them in blood, and nearly all of them in social constitution, descended from the owners of the Roman Villas which had seen the petty but recurrent pirate invasions of the fifth and sixth centuries.

But though the manorial arrangement, with its village lords and their dependent serfs, was common to the whole of the West, and could be found on the Rhine, in Gaul, and even in Italy, in Saxon England it had this peculiarity, that there was no systematic organisation by which the local landowner definitely recognised a feudal superior, and through him the power of a Central Government. Or rather, though in theory such recognition had grown up towards the end of the Saxon period, in practice it hardly existed, and when William landed the whole system of tenure was in disorder, in the sense that the local lord of the village was not accustomed to the interference of a superior, and that no groups of lords had come into existence by which the territorial system could be bound in sheaves, as it were, and the whole of it attached to one central point at the royal Court.

Such a system of groups *had* arisen in Gaul, and to that difference ultimately we owe the French territorial system of the present day, but William the Norman's new subjects had no comprehension of it.

It was upon this account that even those manors which he handed over to his French kindred and dependants were scattered, and that, though he framed a vigorous feudal rule centring in his own hands, the ancient customs of the populace, coupled with the lack of any bond between scattered and locally independent units, forbade that rule to endure.

William's order was not a century old when the recrudescence of the former manorial independence was felt in the reign of Henry II. Under the personal unpopularity of his son, John, it blazed out into successful revolt, and, in spite of the veil thrown over underlying and permanent customs by such strong feudal kings as the first and the third Edwards, the independence and power of the village landlord remained the chief and growing character of English life. It expressed itself in the quality of the local English Parliament, in the support of the usurping Lancastrian dynasty – in twenty ways that converge and mingle towards the close of the Middle Ages.

But after the Dissolution of the monasteries this power of the squires takes on quite a different complexion: the landowning class, from a foundation for the National Government, became, within two generations of the Dissolution, the master of that Government.

For many centuries previous to the sixteenth the old funded wealth of the Crown had been gradually wasting, at the expense of the Central National Government and to the profit of the squires. But the alienation was never complete. There are plenty of cases in which the Crown is found resuming the proprietorship of a manor to which it had never abandoned the theoretical title. With the Tudors such cases become rarer and rarer, with the Stuarts they cease.

The cause of this rapid enfeeblement of the Crown lay largely in the changed proportion of wealth. The King, until the middle of the sixteenth century, had been far wealthier than any one of his subjects. By a deliberate act, the breaking up of ecclesiastical tenure, the Crown offered an opportunity to the wealthier of those subjects so enormously to increase their revenues as to overshadow itself; in a little more than a century after the throwing open of the monastic lands the King is an embarrassed individual, with every issue of expenditure ear-marked, every source of it controlled, and his very person, as it were, mortgaged to a plutocracy. The squires had not only added to their revenues the actual amounts produced by the sites and estates of the old religious foundations, they had been able by this sudden accession of wealth to shoot ahead in their competition with their fellow-citizens. The *counterweight* to the power of the local landlord disappeared with the disappearance of the monastery.

To show how the religious houses had furnished a powerful counterweight by which the Central Government and the populace could continue to oppose the growing power of the landed oligarchy, we may take all the southern bank of the Thames from Buscot to Windsor. We find at the time of the Conquest twelve royal manors and fifteen religious; only the nine remaining were under private lords. Four and a half centuries later, at the time of the Dissolution, the royal manors have passed for the most part into private hands, but the manors in the hands of the religious houses have actually increased in number.

At this point it is important to note an economic phenomenon which appears at first sight accidental, but which, on examination, is found to spring from calculable political

causes. At the moment of the Dissolution it was apparently
in the power of the Crown to have concentrated the revenues of all these monastic manors into its own hands, and
this typical stretch of country, the Berkshire shore, shows
how economically powerful the Central Government of
England might have become had the property surrendered
to the Crown been kept in the hands of the King.

The modern reader will be tempted to inquire why it
was not so kept.

Most certainly Henry intended to keep, if not the whole
of it (for he must reward his servants, and he was accustomed to do things largely), yet at least the bulk of it in
the Royal Treasury, and had he been able to do so the
Central Government of England would have become by
far the strongest thing in Europe. It is conceivable, though
in consideration of the national character doubtful, that
with so powerful an instrument of government, England,
instead of standing aside from the rapid bureaucratic recast-
ing of European civilisation which was the work of the
French Crown, might have led the way in that chief of
modern experiments. One can imagine the Stuarts, had
they possessed revenue, doing what the Bourbons did: one
can imagine the modern State developing under an English
Crown wealthier than any other European Government,
and the re-birth of Europe happening just to the north,
instead of just to the south, of the Channel.

But the speculation is vain. As a fact, the whole of the
new wealth slipped rapidly from between the fingers of the
English King.

When of three forces which still form an equilibrium

two are stationary and one is pressing upon these two, then, if either of the stationary forces be removed, that which was pressing upon both overwhelms the stationary force that remains. The monastic system had been marking time for over 100 years, and in certain political aspects of its power had perhaps slightly dwindled. The monarchy, for all its splendour, was in actual resources no more than it had been for some generations. Pressing upon either of these two institutions was the rising and still rising force of the squires. It is not wonderful that under such conditions the spoil fell to the younger and advancing power.

Consider, for example, the extraordinary anxiety of so apparently powerful a king as Henry for the formal consent of the Commons to his acts. It has been represented as part of the Tudor national policy and what not, but those who write thus have not perhaps smiled, as has the present writer, over the names of those who sat for the English shires in the Parliament which assented to the Dissolution of the great monastic houses. Here is a Ratcliffe from Northumberland, and a Collingwood; here is a Dacre, a Musgrave, a Blenkinsop; the Constables are there, and the Nevilles from Yorkshire; the Tailboys of Lincoln, a Schaverell, a Throgmorton, a Ferrers, a Gascoyne; and of course, inevitably, sitting for Bedfordshire, a hungry Russell.

Here is a Townshend, a Wingfield, a Wentworth, an Audley – all from East Anglia – a Butler; from Surrey a Carew, and that FitzWilliam whose appetite for the religious spoils proved so insatiable; here is a Blount out of Shropshire; a Lyttleton, a Talbot (and yet *another* Russell!), a Darrell, a Paulet, a Courtney (to see what could be picked up in his native county of Devon), and after him a Grenfell. These are a few names taken at random to show what humble sort of 'Commons' it was that Henry had to consider. They are significant names; and the 'Constitution' had little to do then, and has little to do now, with their domination. Wealth was and is their instrument of power.

That such men could ultimately force the Government is evident, but what is remarkable, perhaps, is the extraordinary rapidity with which the Crown was stripped of its new wealth by the gentry, and this can only be explained in two ways:

First, there was the rapid change in prices which rose from the Spanish importation of precious metals from America, the effect of which was now reaching England; and, secondly, the Tudor character.

As to the first, it put the National Government, dependent as it still largely was upon the customary and fixed payments, into a perpetual embarrassment. Where it still received nothing but the customary shilling, it had to pay out three for material and wages, whose price had risen and was rising. In this embarrassment, in spite of every subterfuge and shift, the Crown was in perpetual, urgent, and increasing need. Rigid and novel taxes were imposed, loans were raised and not repaid, but something far more was needed to save the situation, with prices still rising as the years advanced. Ready money from those already in possession of perhaps half the arable land of England was an obvious source, and into their pockets flowed, as by the force of gravitation, the funded wealth which had once supported the old religion. Hardly ever at more than ten years' purchase, sometimes at far less, the Crown turned its new rentals into ready money, and spent that capital as though it had been income.

The Tudor character was a second cause.

It is a pleasing speculation to conceive that, if some character other than a Tudor had been upon the throne, not all at least of this national inheritance would have been dissipated. One can imagine a character – tenacious, pure, narrow and subtle, intent upon dignity, and with a natural suspicion of rivals – which might have saved some part of the estates for posterity. Charles I, for example, had he been born 100 years earlier, might very well have done the thing.

But the Tudors, for all their violence, were fundamentally weak. There was always some vice or passion to interrupt the continuity of their policy – even Mary, who was not the offspring of caprice, had inherited the mental taint of the Spanish house – and before the last of the family had died, while still old men were living who, as children, had seen the monasteries, nearly all this vast treasure had found its way into the pockets of the squires. In the middle of the seventeenth century every one of these villages is under a private landlord: before the close of it even the theoretical link of their feudal dependence upon the Crown is snapped: and the two centuries between that time and our own have seen the power of the new landlords steadily maintained and latterly vastly increased.

Apart from the transfer of the monastic manors there was yet another way in which the Dissolution of the religious houses helped on the establishment of the landed oligarchy in the place of the old National Government. The monasteries had owned not only these full manorial rights, but also numerous parcels of land scattered up and down in manors whose lordship was already in private hands. These parcels, like the small lay freeholds, which they resembled, formed nuclei of resistance to the increasing power of the squires.

The point is of very considerable importance, though not easy to seize for anyone unacquainted with the way in which the territorial oligarchy has been built up or ignorant of the present conditions of English village life.

At the close of the Middle Ages the lord of a manor in England, though possessed of a larger proportion of the land than were his colleagues in other countries, but rarely could claim so much as one half of the acreage of a parish; the rest was common, in which his rights were strictly limited and defined, to the advantage of the poor, and also side by side with common was to be found a number of partially and wholly independent tenures, over which the squire had little or no control, from copyholds which did furnish him occasional sums of money, to freeholds which were practically independent of him.

The monasteries possessed parcels of this sort everywhere. To give but one example: Chertsey had twenty acres of freehold pasturage in the Manor of Cobham; but it is useless to give examples of a thing which was as common as the renting of a house to-day. Now these small parcels formed a most valuable foundation upon which the independence of similar lay parcels could repose. The squire might be tempted to bully a four-acre man out of his land, but he could not bully the Abbot of Abingdon, or of Reading. And so long as these small parcels were sanctioned by the power of the great houses, so long they were certain to endure in the hands even of the smallest and the humblest of the tenants. To-day in a modern village where a gentleman possesses such an island of land, better still where several do, there at once arises a tendency and an opportunity for the smaller men to acquire and to retain. The present writer could quote a Sussex village in the centre of which were to be found, but thirty years ago, more than half-a-dozen freeholds. They disappeared: in its prosperity 'The Estate' extinguished them. The next heir in his embarrassment has handed over the whole lump to a Levantine for a loan. Had the Old Squire spared the small freeholds they would have come in as purchasers and would have increased their number during the later years when the principal landlord, his son, was gradually falling into poverty and drink.

When the monasteries were gone the disappearance of the small men gradually began. It was hastened by the extinction of that old tradition which made the Church a customary landlord exacting quit rents always less than the economic value of the land, and, what with the security of tenure and the low rental, creating a large tenant right. This tenant right vested in the lucky dependants of the Church did indeed create intense local jealousies that help to account for much of the antagonism to the monastic houses. But the future showed that the benefits conferred, though irregular and privileged, were more than the landless men could hope to expect when they had exchanged the monk for the squire.

Finally, the Dissolution of the religious houses strengthened the squires in the mere machinery of the constitution.
Before that Dissolution the House of Lords was a clerical
house. Had you entered the Council of Henry VII when
Parliament sat at Westminster you would have seen a crowd
of mitres and of croziers, bishops and abbots of the great
abbeys, among whom, here and there, were some thirty lay
lords. This clerical House of Lords, sprung largely from the
populace, possessed only of life tenure, was a very different thing from the House of Lords that succeeded the
Dissolution. *That* immediately became a committee, as it
were, of the landed class; and a committee of the landed
class the House of Lords remained until quite the last few
years, when the practice of purchase has admitted to it
brewers, money-lenders, Colonial speculators, and, indeed,
anyone who can furnish the sum required by a woman or
a secret party fund. A concrete example is often of value
in the illustration of a general process, and at the expense
of a digression I propose to lay before the reader as excellent a picture as we have of the way in which the Dissolution of the monasteries not only emphasised the position
of the existing territorial class, but began to recruit it with
elements drawn from every quarter, and, while it established the squires in power, taught them to be careless of
the origin or of the end of the families admitted to their
rank.

For this purpose I can find no better example than that
of the family of Williams, which by the licence of custom
we have come to call 'Cromwell'; the most famous member
of this family stands out in English history as the typical

squire who led the Forces of his Order against the impoverished Monarchy, and so reduced that emblem of Government to the simulacrum which it still remains.

Putney, by Thames-side, was the home of their very lowly beginnings.

Of the descent of the Williams throughout the Middle Ages nothing is known. Much later they claimed relationship with certain heads of the Welsh clans, but the derivation is fantastic. At any rate a certain Williams was keeping a public-house in Putney in the generation which saw the first of the Reformers. His name was Morgan, and the 'Ap William' or 'Williams' which he added to that name was an affix due to the Welsh custom of calling a man by his father's name; for surnames had not yet become a rule in the Principality. He may have come, and probably did, from Glamorganshire, and that is all we can say about him; though we must admit some weight in Leland's contemporary evidence that his son, Richard, was born in the same county, at a place called Llanishen. Anyhow, there he is, keeping his public-house in the first years of the sixteenth century by the riverside at Putney.

There lived in the same hamlet (which was a dependency of the manor of Wimbledon) a certain Cromwell or Crumwell, who was also called Smith; but this obscure personage should most probably be known by the first of these two names, for his humble business was the shoeing of horses, and the second appellation was very probably a nickname arising from that trade. He also added beer-selling to his other work, and this common occupation may have formed a link between him and his neighbour, Morgan ap William.

The next stage in the story is not perfectly clear. Smith or Crumwell had a son and two daughters, the son was called Thomas, and the daughter that concerns us was called Katherine. It is highly probable, according to modern research into the records of the manor, that Morgan ap William married Katherine. But the matter is still in some doubt. There are not a few authorities, some of them painstaking, though all of them old, who will have it that the blacksmith's son, Thomas, loved Morgan ap William's sister, instead of its being the other way about. It is not easy to establish the exact relationship between two public-house keepers who lived as neighbours in a dirty little village 400 years ago.

Thomas proceeded to an astonishing career; he left his father's forge, wandered to Italy, may have been present at the sack of Rome, and was at last established as a merchant in the city of London. When one says 'merchant' one is talking kindly. His principal business then, as throughout his life, was that of a usurer, and he showed throughout his incredible adventures something of that mixture of simplicity and greed, with a strange fixity in the oddest of personal friendships, which amuses us to-day in our company promoters and African adventurers. His abilities recommended him to Wolsey, and when that great genius fell, Cromwell was, as the most familiar of historical traditions represents him, faithful to his master.

Whether this faithfulness recommended him to the King or not, it is difficult to say. Probably it did, for there is nothing that a careful plotter will more narrowly watch in an agent than his record of fidelity in the past.

Henry fixed upon him to be his chief instrument in the suppression of the monasteries. His lack of all fixed principle, his unusual power of application to a particular task, his devotion to whatever orders he chose to obey, and his quite egregious avarice, all fitted him for the work his master ordered.

How the witty scoundrel accomplished that business is a matter of common history. Had he never existed the monasteries would have fallen just the same, perhaps in the same manner, and probably with the same despatch. But fate has chosen to associate this revolution with his name – and to his presence in that piece of confiscation we owe the presence in English history of the great Oliver; for Oliver, as will be presently seen, and all his tribe were fed upon no other food than the possessions of the Church. Cromwell, in his business of suppressing the great houses, embezzled quite cynically – if we can fairly call that 'embezzlement' which was probably countenanced by the King, to whom account was due. Indeed, it is plainly evident from the whole story of that vast economic catastrophe which so completely separates the England we know from the England of a thousand years – the England of Alfred, of Edward I, of Chaucer, and of the French Wars – it is evident from the whole story, that the flood of confiscated wealth which poured into the hands of the King's agents and squires was a torrent almost impossible to control; Henry VIII was glad enough to be able to retain, even for a year or two, one half of the spoils.

We know, for instance, that the family of Howard (which was then already of more than a century's standing) took everything they could lay their hands on in the particular case of Bridlington – pyxes, chalices, crucifixes, patens, reliquaries, vestments, shrines, every saleable or meltable thing, and the cattle and pigs into the bargain, and never dreamt of giving account to the King.

With Cromwell, the embezzlement was more systematic: it was a method of keeping accounts. But our interest lies in the fact that the process was accompanied by that curious fidelity to all with whom he was personally connected, which forms so interesting a feature in the sardonic character of this adventurer. It is here that we touch again upon the family of Morgan ap William, the public-house keeper of Putney.

When Cromwell was at the height of his power he lifted out from the obscurity of his native kennel a certain Richard Williams, calling him now 'cousin' and now 'nephew'. We may take it that the boy was a nephew, and that the word 'cousin' was used only in the sense of general relationship which attached to it at that time. If Cromwell had been a man of a trifle more distinction, or of tolerable honesty, we might even be certain that this young fellow was the legitimate son of his sister Katherine, and, indeed, it is much the more probable conclusion at which we should arrive to-day. But Cromwell himself obscured the matter by alluding to his relative as 'Williams (alias Cromwell)', and there must necessarily remain a suspicion as to the birth and real status of his dependant.

In 1538 this young Richard Williams got two foundations handed over to him – both in Huntingdon, and together amounting in value to about £500 a year.

We have seen on an earlier page how extremely difficult or impossible it is to estimate exactly in modern money the figures of the Dissolution. We have agreed that to multiply by twenty for a maximum is permissible, but that even then we shall not have anything like the true relation of any particular income to the general standard of wealth in a time when England was so much smaller than our England of to-day, and in an England where wealth had been until that moment so well divided, and especially in an England where the objects both of luxury and expenditure were so utterly different to our own: where all textile fabric was, for instance, so much dearer in proportion to food than it is now, and where yet a man could earn in a few weeks' labour what would with us be capital enough to stock a small farm.

It is safe to say, however, that when Cromwell had got his young relation – whatever that relationship was – into possession of the two foundations in Huntingdon, he had set him up as a considerable local gentleman, and whether it was the inheritance of the Cromwell blood through his mother, or something equally unpleasant in the heredity of his father, Morgan, young Williams ('alias Cromwell') did not stick there.

Early in 1540 he swallowed bodily the enormous revenues of Ramsey Abbey.

Now to appreciate what that meant we must return to the case we have already established in the case of Westminster. Westminster almost alone of the great foundations remains with a certain splendour attached to it; we cannot, indeed, see all the dependencies as they used to stand to the south of the great Abbey. We cannot see the lively and populous community dependent upon it; still less can we appreciate what a figure it must have cut in the days when London was but a large country town, and when this walled monastic community stood in its full grandeur surrounded by its gardens and farms. But still, the object lesson afforded by the Abbey yet remains visible to us. We can see it as it was, and we know that its income must have represented in the England at that time infinitely more in outward effect than do to-day the largest private incomes of our English gentry: a Solomon Joel, for instance, or a Rothschild, does not occupy so great a place in modern England as did Westminster, at the close of the Middle Ages, in the very different England of its time.

Well, Ramsey was the equivalent of half Westminster, and young Williams swallowed it whole. He was not given it outright, but the price at which he bought it is significant of the way in which the monastic lands were distributed, and in which incidentally the squirearchy of England was founded. He bought it for less than three years' purchase. Where he got the money, or indeed whether he paid ready money at all, we do not know. If he did furnish the sum down we may suspect that he borrowed it from his uncle, and we may hope that that genial financier charged but a low rate of interest to one whom he had so signally favoured.

Contemporaneously with this vast accession of fortune, which made Williams the principal man in the county, Cromwell, now Earl of Essex, fell from favour, and was executed. The barony was revived for his son five months after his death and was not extinguished until the first years of the eighteenth century, but with this, the direct lineage of the King's Vicar-General, we are not concerned: our business is with the family of Williams.

Young Williams did not imitate his protector in showing any startling fidelity to the fallen. He became a courtier, was permanently in favour with the King and with the King's son, and died established in the great territorial position which he had come into by so singular an accident.

His son, Henry, maintained that position, and possibly increased it. He was four times High Sheriff of the two counties; he received Elizabeth, his sovereign and patroness, at his seat at Hinchinbrooke (one of the convents), and in general he played the rôle with which we are so tediously familiar in the case of the new and monstrous fortunes of our own times.

He was in Parliament also for the Queen, and it was his brother who moved the resolution of thanks to Elizabeth for the beheading of Mary Queen of Scots.

He died in 1603, and even to his death the alias was maintained. 'Williams (alias Cromwell)' was the legal signature which guaranteed the validity of purchases and sales, while to the outer world CROMWELL (alias Williams) was the formula by which the family gently thrust itself into the tradition of another and more genteel name. The whole thing was done, like everything else this family ever did, by a mixture of trickery and patience; he obtained no special leave from Chancery as the law required; he simply used the 'Williams' in public less and less and the 'Cromwell' more and more. When he died, his sons after him, Robert and Oliver, had forgotten the Williams altogether – in public

– and in the case of such powerful men it was convenient for the neighhours to forget the lineage also; so with the end of the sixteenth century these Williams have become Cromwells, *pur et simple*, and Cromwells they remain. But still the old caution clings to them where the law, and especially where money, is concerned; even Robert's son, who grew to be the Lord Protector, signs *Williams* when it is a case of securing his wife's dowry. Of Robert and Oliver, sons of Henry, and grandsons of the original Richard, Oliver, the elder, inherited, of course, the main wealth of the family, but Robert also was portioned, and as was invariably the case with the Williams' (alias Cromwell), the portion took the form of monastic lands.

Many more estates of the Church had come into the hands of this highly accretive family in the half century that had passed since the destruction of the monasteries. Thus at the very end of the century we find Oliver selling the abbey land of Stratton to a haberdasher in London for £3000.

The portion of this younger brother, Robert, consisted of religious estates in the town of Huntingdon itself, and it is highly characteristic of the whole tribe that the very house in which the Lord Protector was born was monastic, and had been, before the Dissolution, a hospital dedicated to the use of the poor. For the Lord Protector was the son of this Robert, who by a sort of atavism had added to the ample income derived from monastic spoil the profits of a brewery. It was Mrs Cromwell who looked after the brewery, and some appreciable part of the family revenues were derived from it when, in 1617, her husband died, leaving young Oliver, the future Lord Protector, an only son of eighteen, upon her hands.

The quarrels between young Oliver and old Oliver (the absurdly wealthy head of the family) would furnish material for several diverting pages, but they do not concern this, which is itself but a digression from the general subject of my book.

The object of that digression has been to trace the growth of but one great territorial family, from the gutter to affluence in the course of less than 100 years; to show how plain 'Williams' gradually and secretly became 'Cromwell' – because the new name had about it a flavour of nobility, however parvenu; to show how the whole of their vast revenues depended upon, and was born from, the destruction of monastic system, and to show by the example of one Thames-side family how rapidly and from what sources was derived that economic power of the squires which, when it came to the issue of arms, utterly destroyed what was left of the national monarchy.

The new *régime* had, however, other features about it which must not be forgotten. For instance, in this growth of a new territorial body upon the ruins of the monastic orders, in this sudden and portentous increase of the wealth and power of the squires of England, the mutability of the new system is perhaps as striking as any other of its characteristics.

Manors or portions of manors which had been steadily fixed in the possession and customs of these undying corporations for centuries pass rapidly from hand to hand, and though there is sometimes a lull in the process the uprooting reoccurs after each lull, as though continuity and a strong tradition, which are necessarily attached for good or for evil to a free peasantry, were as necessarily disregarded by a landed plutocracy. There is not, perhaps, in all Europe a similar complete carelessness for the traditions of the soil and for the attachment of a family to an ancestral piece of land as is to be found among these few thousand squires. The system remains, but the individual families, the particular lineages, appear without astonishment and are destroyed almost without regret. Aliens, Orientals and worse, enter the ruling class, and are received without surprise; names that recall the Elizabethans go out, and are not mourned.

We are accustomed to-day, when we see some village estate in our own country pass from an impoverished gentleman to some South African Jew, to speak of the passing of an old world and of its replacement by a new and a worse one. But an examination of the records which follow the Dissolution of the monasteries may temper our sorrow. The wound that was dealt in the sixteenth century to our general national traditions affected the love of the land as profoundly as it did religion, and the apparent antiquity which the trees, the stones, and a certain spurious social feeling lend to these country houses is wholly external.

Among the riparian manors of the Thames the fate of Bisham is very characteristic of the general fate of monastic land. It was surrendered, among other smaller monasteries, in 1536, though it enjoyed an income corresponding to about £6000 a year of our money, and of course very much more than £6000 a year in our modern way of looking at incomes. It was thus a wealthy place, and how it came to be included in the smaller monasteries is not quite clear.

At any rate it was restored immediately after. The monks of Chertsey were housed in it, as we have already seen, and the revenues of several of the smaller dissolved houses were added to it; so that it was at the moment of its refoundation about three times as wealthy as it had been before. The prior who had surrendered in 1536, one Barlow, was made Bishop of St Asaphs, and in turn of St Davids, Bath and Wells, and Chichester; he is that famous Barlow who took the opportunity of the Reformation to marry, and whose five daughters all in turn married the Protestant bishops of the new Church of England. But this is by the way. The fate of the land is what is interesting. From Anne of Cleves, whose portion it had been, and to whom the Government of the great nobles under Edward VI confirmed it after Henry VIII's death, it passed, upon her surrendering it in 1552, to a certain Sir Philip Hoby. He had been of the Privy Council of Henry VIII. Upon his death it passed to his nephew, Edward Hoby; Edward was a Parliamentarian under Elizabeth, wrote on Divinity, and left an illegitimate son, Peregrine, to whom he bequeathed Bisham upon his death in 1617. It need hardly be said that before 100 years were over the son was already legitimatised in the county traditions; his son, Edward, was created Baron just after the Restoration, in 1666. The succession was kept up for just 100 years more, when the last male heir of the family died in 1766. He was not only a baron but a parson as well, and on his death the estate went to relatives by the name of Mill, or, as we might imagine, 'Hoby' Mill. It did not long remain with them. They died out in 1780 and the Van Sittarts bought it of the widow.

Consider Chertsey, from which Bisham sprang. The utter dispersion of the whole tradition of Chertsey is more violent than that perhaps of any other historical site in England. The Crown maintained, as we have seen to be the case elsewhere, its nominal hold upon the foundations of the abbey and of what was left of the buildings, though that hold was only nominal, and it maintained such a position until 1610 – that is, for a full lifetime after the community was dispersed. But the tradition created by FitzWilliam continued, and the Crown was ready to sell at that date, to a certain Dr. Hammond. The perpetual mobility which seems inseparable from spoils of this kind attaches thenceforward to the unfortunate place. The Hammonds sell after the Restoration to Sir Nicholas Carew, and before the end of the seventeenth century the Carews pass it on to the Orbys, and the Orbys pass it on to the Waytes. The Waytes sell it to a brewer of London, one Hinde. So far, contemptuous as has been the treatment of this great national centre, it had at least remained intact. With Hinde's son even that dignity deserted it. He found it advisable to distribute the land in parcels as a speculation; the actual emplacement of the building went to a certain Harwell, an East Indian, in 1753, and his son left it by will to a private soldier called Fuller, who was suspected of being his illegitimate brother. Fuller, as might be expected, saw nothing but an opportunity of making money. He redivided what was left intact of the old estate, and sold that again by lots in 1809; a stockbroker bought the remaining materials of a house whose roots struck back to the very footings of our country, sold them for what they were worth – and there was the end of Chertsey.

Then there is also Radley: which begins as an exception, but fails. It was a manor of Abingdon, and after the Dissolution it fell a prey to that one of the Seymours who proved too dirty and too much even for his brother and was put to death in 1549. It passed for the moment, as we have seen several of these riverside manors do, into the hands of Mary. But upon her death Elizabeth bestowed it upon a certain Stonehouse, and the Stonehouses did come uncommonly near to founding a family that should endure. Nor can their tradition be said to have disappeared when the name changed and the manor passed to the nephew of the last Stonehouse, by name Bowyer. But Bowyer did not retain it. He gradually ruined himself: and it is amusing at this distance of time to learn that the cause of his ruin was the idea that coal underlay his property. Everyone knows what Radley since became: it was purchased by an enthusiast, and is now a school springing from his foundation.

Or consider the two Hinkseys opposite Oxford, both portions of Abingdon manors; they are granted in the general loot to two worthies bearing the names of Owen and Bridges: a doctor.

These were probably no more than vulgar speculators upon a premium – 'Stags', as we should say to-day – for a few years afterwards we find a Williams in possession of one of the Hinkseys; he is followed by the Perrots, and only quite late, and by purchase, do we come to the somewhat more dignified name of Harcourt. The other Hinksey, after still more varied adventures, ends up in the hands of the Berties, obscure south-country people who date from a rich Protestant marriage of the time.

Cholsey, again, with its immemorial traditions of unchanging ecclesiastical custom, receiving its priests in Saxon times from the Mont St Michel upon the marches of Brittany, and later holding as a manor from the Abbot of Reading, remains with the Crown but a very few years. In 1555 Mary handed it over to that Sir Robert Englefield who was promptly attainted by her successor. It gets in the hands of the Knowleses, then of the Riches, and ends up with the family of Edwardes – seventeenth-century Welshmen, who, by a plan of wealthy marriages, became gentlemen, and have now for 100 years and more been peers, under the title of Kensington.

The mention of Sir Robert Englefield leads one to what is perhaps the best example in the whole Thames Valley of this perpetual chop and change in the holding of English land; that example is to be discovered at Pangbourne.

Pangbourne also was monastic; and the manor held, as did Cholsey, of Reading Abbey. In the race for the spoils Dudley clutched it in 1550. When he was beheaded, three years later, and it passed again to the Crown, Mary handed it (as she had handed Cholsey) to Sir Robert Englefield. His attainder followed. Within ten years it changes hands again. Elizabeth in 1563 gave it to her cofferer, a Mr Weldon. This personage struck no root, nor his son after him, for in 1613, while still some were alive who could remember the old custom and immemorial monastic lordship of the place, Weldon the younger sold it to a certain Davis.

Davis, one would hope – in that seventeenth century which was so essentially the century of the squires, and in that generation also wherein the squires wiped out what was left of the Crown and left the King a salaried dependant of the governing class – Davis might surely have attempted to found a family and to achieve some sort of dignity of tradition. He probably made no such an attempt, but if he did he failed; for only half-a-century later the unfortunate place changes hands again, and the Davises sell it to the Breedons.

The Breedons showed greater stability. They are actually associated with Pangbourne for over a century, but even this experiment in lineage broke down, through the extinction of the direct line. In 1776, by a sham continuity consonant to the whole recent story of English land, it passes to yet another family on the condition of their assuming the name of Breedon – which was not their own.

All up and down England, and especially in this Thames Valley, which is in all its phases so typical and symbolical of the rest of the country, this stir and change of tenure is to be found, originating with the sharp changes of 1540, and continuing to our own day.

Anywhere along this Berkshire shore of the Thames the process may be traced; even the poor little ruined nunnery of Ankerwike shows it. The site of that quiet and forgotten community was seized under Edward VI by Smith the courtier. Then you find it in the pockets of the Salters, after them of the Lysons. The Lysons sell it to the Lees, and finally it passes by marriage to the Harcourts.

The number of such examples that could be taken in the Valley of the Thames alone would be far too cumbersome for these pages. One can close the list with Sonning.

Sonning, which had been very possibly the see of an

early bishopric, and which was certainly a country house of the Bishop of Salisbury, did not pass from ecclesiastical hands by a theft, but it was none the less doomed to the same mutability as the rest. In 1574 it was exchanged with the Crown for lands in Dorset. The Crown kept it for an unusually long time, considering the way in which land slipped on every side from the control of the National Government at this period. It is still royal under Charles I, but it passes in 1628 to Halstead and Chamberlain. In little more than twenty years it is in the hands of the family of Rich. Then there is a lull, just as there was in the case of Pangbourne, and a continuity that lasts throughout the eighteenth century. But just as a tradition began to form it was broken, and in the first years of the nineteenth century Sonning is sold to the Palmers.

Parallel to the rise of the squires and their capture of English government has gone the development of the English town system. And this, the last historical phase with which we shall deal in these pages, is also very well and typically illustrated in the history of the Thames Valley. That valley contains London, which is, of course, not only far the largest but in its way the fullest example of what is peculiarly English in the development of town life; and it contains, in the modern rise of Oxford and Reading, two of the very best instances to show how the English town in its modern aspect has sprung from the industrial system and from the introduction of railways. For neither has any natural facilities for production, and the growth of each in the nineteenth century has been wholly artificial.

The most recent change of all, with which these notes

will end, is, one need hardly say, this industrial transformation. It has made a completely new England, and it nourishes the only civilised population in the world which is out of touch with arms, and with the physical life and nature of the country it inhabits, and the only population in which the vast majority are concerned with things of which they have no actual experience, and feel most strongly upon matters dictated to them at second or third hand by the proprietors of great journals.

What that new England will become none of us can tell; we cannot even tell whether the considerable problem of maintaining it as an organised civilisation will or will not be solved. All the conditions are so completely new, our whole machinery of government so thoroughly presupposes a little aristocratic agricultural state, and our strong attachment to form and ritual so hampers all attempts at reorganisation, that the way in which we shall answer, if we do answer, the question of this sphinx, cannot as yet even be guessed at.

But long before the various historical causes at work had begun to produce the great modern English town, long before the use of coal, the development of the navy, and, above all, the active political transformation of our rivals during the eighteenth century, had given us that industrial supremacy which we have but recently lost, the English town was a thing with characteristics of its own in Europe.

In the first place, it was not municipal in the Roman sense. The sharp distinction which the Roman Empire and the modern French Republic, and, from the example of that republic, the whole of Western Europe, establish between town and country, comes from the fact that European thought, method of government, and the rest, were formed on the Mediterranean: but the civilisation of the Mediterranean was one of city states; the modern civilisation which has returned to Roman traditions is, therefore, necessarily municipal. A man's first country in antiquity was his town; he died for his town; he left his wealth to his town; the word 'civilisation', like the word 'citizen', and like a hundred words connected with the superiority of mankind, are drawn from the word for a town. To be political, to possess a police, to recognise boundaries – all this was to be a townsman, and the various districts of the Empire took their proper names, at least, from the names of their chief cities, as do to-day the French and the Italian countrysides.

Doubtless in Roman times the governing forces of Britain attempted a similar system here. But it does not seem ever to have taken root in the same way that it did beyond the Channel. The absence of a municipal system in the fullest sense is one of the very few things which differentiates the Roman Britain from the rest of the Empire, others being a land frontier to the west, and the large survival of aboriginal dialects.

The Roman towns were not small, indeed Roman London was very large; they were not ill connected with highroads; they were certainly wealthy and full of commerce; but they gave their names to no districts, and their municipal institutions have left but very faint traces upon posterity.

The barbarian invasions fell severely upon the Roman cities of Britain, in some very rare cases they may have been actually destroyed, but in the much more numerous cases where we may be reasonably sure that municipal life continued without a break throughout the incursions of the pirates, their decay was pitiful; and when recorded history begins again, after a gap of two hundred years, with the Roman missionaries of the sixth and seventh centuries, we find thenceforward, and throughout the Saxon period, many of the towns living the life of villages.

The proportion that were walled was much smaller than was the case upon the Continent, and even the most enduring emblem and the most tenacious survival of the Roman Imperial system – namely, the Bishop seated in the chief municipality of his district – was not universal to English life.

It is characteristic of Gregory the Great that he intended, or is believed to have intended, Britain, when he had recivilised it, to be set out upon a clear Latin model, with a Primate in the chief city and suffragans in every other. But if he had such a plan (and it would have been a typically Latin plan) he must have been thinking of a Britain very different from that which his envoys actually found. When the work was accomplished the little market town of Canterbury was the seat of the Primate; the old traditions of York secured for it a second archbishop, great London could not be passed over, but small villages in some places, insignificant boroughs in others, were the sites of cathedrals. Selsey, a rural manor or fishing hamlet, was the episcopal centre of St Wilfrid and his successors in their government of Sussex; Dorchester, as we have seen, was the episcopal town, or rather village, for something like half England. In the names of its officers also and in the methods of their government the Anglo-Saxon town was agricultural.

With the advent of the Normans, as one might expect, municipal life to some extent re-arose. But it still maintained its distinctively English character throughout the Middle Ages. Contrast London or Oxford, for instance, in the twelfth and early thirteenth centuries, with contemporary Paris. In London and Oxford the wall is built once for all, and when it is completed the town may grow into suburbs as much as it likes, no new wall is built. In Paris, throughout its history, as the town grows, the first concern of its Government is to mark out new limits which shall sharply define it from the surrounding country. Philip Augustus does it, a century and a half later Etienne Marcel did it; through the seventeenth century, and the eighteenth, the custom is continued: through the nineteenth also, and to-day new and strict limits are about to be imposed on the expanded city.

Again the metropolitan idea, which is consonant to, and the climax of, a municipal system, is absent from the story of English towns.

Until a good hundred years after the Conquest you cannot say where the true capital of England is, and when you find it at last in London, the King's Court is in a suburb outside the walls and the Parliament of a century later yet meets at Westminster and not in the City.

The English judges are not found fixed in local municipal centres, they are itinerant. The later organisation of the Peace does not depend upon the county towns; it is an organisation of rural squires; and, most significant of all, no definite distinction can ever be drawn between the English village and the English town neither in spirit nor in legal definition. You have a town like Maidenhead, which has a full local Government, and yet which has no mayor for centuries. Conversely, a town having once had a mayor may dwindle down into a village, and no one who respects English tradition bothers to interfere with the anomaly. For instance, you may to-day in Orford enjoy the hospitality, or incur the hostility, of a Mayor and Corporation.

On all these accounts the banks of the Thames, until quite the latest part of our historical development, presented a line of settlements in which it was often difficult to draw the distinction between the village and the town.

Consider also this characteristic of the English thing, that the boroughs sending Members to Parliament first sent them quite haphazard and then by prescription.

Simon de Montfort gets just a few borough Members to his Parliament because he knows they will be on his side; and right down to the Tudors places are enfranchised – as, for example, certain Cornish boroughs were – not because they are true towns but because they will support the Government. Once returning Members, the place has a right to return them, until the partial reform of 1832. It is a right like the hereditary right of a peer, a quaint custom. It has no relation to municipal feeling, for municipal feeling does not exist. Old Sarum may lose every house, Gatton may retain but seven freeholders, yet each solemnly returns its two Members to Parliament.

From the first records that we possess until the beginning of the nineteenth century, the line of the Thames was a string of large villages and small towns, differing in size and wealth far less than their descendants do to-day.

In this arrangement, of course, the valley was similar to all the rest of England, but perhaps the prosperity of the larger villages and the frequency of the market towns was more marked on the line of the Thames than in any other countryside, from the permanent influx of wealth due to the royal castles, the great monastic foundations, and the continual stream of travel to and from London which bound the whole together.

Cricklade, Lechlade, Oxford, Abingdon, Dorchester, Wallingford, Reading, and Windsor – old Windsor, that is – were considerable places from at least the period of the Danish invasions. They formed the objective of armies, or the subject matter of treaties or important changes. But the first standard of measure which we can apply is that given us by the Norman Survey.

How indecisive is that standard has already been said. We do not accurately know what categories of wealth were registered in Domesday. The Anglo-Saxon Chronicle, barbaric in this as in most other matters, would have it that the Survey was complete, and applied to all the landed fortune of England. That, of course, is absurd. But we do have a rough standard of comparison for rural manors, though it is a very rough one. Though we cannot tell how much of the measurements and of the numbers given are conventional and how much are real, though we do not know whether the plough-lands referred to are real fields or merely measures of capacity for production, though historians are condemned to ceaseless guessing upon every term of the document, and though the last orthodox guess is exploded every five or six years – yet when we are told that one manor possessed so many ploughs or paid upon so many hides, or had so many villein holdings while another manor had but half or less in each category; and when we see the dues, say three times as large in the first as in the second, then we can say with certitude that the first was much more important than the second; *how* much more important we cannot say. We can, to repeat an argument already advanced, affirm the inhabitants of any given manor to be at the very least not less than five times the number of holdings, and thus fix a *minimum* everywhere. For instance, we can be certain that William's rural England had not less than 2 million, though we cannot say how much more they may not have been – 3 million, 4 million, or 5 million. In agricultural life – that is, in the one industry of the time – Domesday does afford a vague statement to the rural conditions of England at the end of the eleventh century, and, dark as it is, no other European nation possesses such a minute record of its economic origins.

But with the towns the case is different. There, except for the minimum of population, we are quite at sea. We may presume that the houses numbered are only the houses paying tax, or at least we may presume this in some cases, but already the local customs of each town were so highly differentiated that it is quite impossible to say with certitude what the figures may mean. It is usual to take the taxable value of the place to the Crown and to establish a comparison on that basis, but it is perhaps wiser, though almost as inconclusive, to consider each case, and all the elements of it separately, and to attempt, by a co-ordination of the different factors given to arrive at some sort of scale.

Judged in this manner, Wallingford and Oxford are the early towns of the Thames Valley which afford the best subjects for survey.

Wallingford in Domesday counted, closes and cottages together, just under 500 units of habitation. It is, of course, a matter of conjecture how much population this would stand for. A minimum is here, as elsewhere, easily established. We may presuppose that a close, even of the largest kind, was but a private one; we may next average the inhabitants of each house at five, which is about the average of modern times, and so arrive at a population of 2500. But this minimum of 2500 for the population of Wallingford at the time of the Conquest is too artificial and too full of modern bias to be received. Not even the strongest prejudice in favour of underrating the wealth and population of early England, a prejudice which has for it objects the emphasising of our modern perfection, would admit so ludicrous a conclusion. But while we may be perfectly certain that the population of Wallingford was far larger than this minimum, to obtain a maximum is not so easy. We do not know, with absolute certainty, whether the whole of the town has been enumerated in the Survey, though we have a better ground for supposing it in this case than in most others. Such numerous details are given of holdings which, though situated in the town, counted in the property of local manors that we are fairly safe in saying that we have here a more than commonly complete survey. The very cottages are mentioned, as, for example, 'twenty-two cottages outside the wall', and their condition is described in terms which, though not easy for us to understand, clearly signify that they could be taken as paying the full tax.

The real elements of uncertainty lie, first, in the number of people normally inhabiting one house at that time, and secondly, in the exact meaning of the word 'haga' or 'close'.

As to the first point, we may take it that one household of five would be the least, ten would be the most, to be present under the roof of an isolated family; but we must remember that the Middle Ages contained in their social system a conception of community which not only appeared (and is still remembered) in connection with monastic institutions, but which inspired the whole of military and civil life. To put it briefly, a man at the time of the Conquest, and for centuries later, would rather have lived as part of a community than as an individual householder, and conversely, those indices of importance and social position which we now estimate in furniture and other forms of ostentation were then to be found in the number of dependants surrounding the head of the house. A merchant, for example, if he flourished, was the head of a very numerous community; every parish church in a town represented a society of priests and of their servants, and of course a garrison (such as Wallingford pre-eminently possessed) meant a very large community indeed. We are usually safe, at any rate in the towns, if we multiply the known number of tenements by ten in order to arrive at the number of souls inhabiting the borough. To give the Wallingford of the Conquest a minimum of 5000, if we were certain that 500 (or, to speak exactly, 491) was the number of single units of taxation within the borough, would be to set that minimum quite low enough.

The second difficulty is that of establishing the meaning of the word 'haga'. In some cases it may represent one single large establishment. But on the other hand we can point to six which between them covered a whole acre, and no one with the least acquaintance of mediæval municipal topography, no one, for instance, who knows the history of twelfth-century Paris, would allow one-sixth of an acre to a single average house within the walls of a town. A close would have one or more wells, it is true; some closes certainly would have gardens, but the labour of fortification, and the privilege of market, were each of them causes which forbade any great extension of open spaces, save in the case of privileged or wealthy communities or individuals.

From what we know of closes elsewhere, it is more probable that these at Wallingford were the 'cells' as it were of the borough organism. A man would be granted in the first growth of the town a unit of land with definitely established boundaries, which he would probably enclose (the word 'haga' refers to such an enclosure), and though at first there might be only one house upon it, it would be to his interest to multiply the tenements within this unit, which unit rendered a regular, customary and unchanging due to its various superiors, whatever the number of inhabitants it grew to contain.

If we turn to a comparison based upon taxation we have equal difficulties, though difficulties of a different sort. We saw in the case of Old Windsor that a community of perhaps 1000, probably of more, but at any rate something more like a large village than a town (and one moreover not rated as a town), paid in dues the equivalent of thirty loads of wheat. Wallingford paid the equivalent of only twenty or twenty-two. But on the other hand the total Farm of the Borough, the globular price at which the taxes could be reckoned upon to yield a profit, was equivalent to no less than 400 such loads.

Judged by the number of hagæ we should have a Wallingford about five times the size of Old Windsor. Judged by the taxable capacity we should have an Old Wallingford of more than ten times the size of Old Windsor.

Here again a further element of complexity enters. It was quite out of the spirit of the Middle Ages to estimate dues, whether to a feudal superior or to the National Government, or even minor payments made to a true proprietorial owner at the full capacity of the economic unit concerned. All such payment was customary. Even where, in the later Middle Ages, a man indubitably owned (in our modern sense of the word 'owned') a piece of freehold land, and let it (in our modern sense of the word 'let'), it would not have occurred to him or his tenant that the very highest price obtainable for the productive capacity of the land should be paid. The philosophy permeating the whole of society compelled the owner and the tenant, even in this extreme case, to a customary arrangement; for it was an arrangement intended to be permanent, to allow for wide fluctuations of value, and therefore to be necessarily a minimum. If this was the case in the later Middle Ages where undoubted proprietary right was concerned, still more was it the case in the early Middle Ages with the customary feudal dues; these varied infinitely from place to place, rising in scale from those of privileged communities wholly exempt to those of places such as we believe Old Windsor to have been, which paid (and these were the exceptions), not indeed every penny that they could pay (as they would now have to pay a modern landlord), but half, or perhaps more than half, such a rent.

Where Wallingford stood in this scale it is quite impossible to say, and we can only conclude with the very general statement that the Wallingford of the Conquest consisted of certainly more than 5000 souls, more probably of 10,000, and quite possibly of more than 10,000.

Having taken Wallingford with its minute and valuable record as a sort of unit, we can roughly compare it with other centres of populations upon the river at the same date.

Old Windsor we have already dealt with, and made it out from a fifth to a tenth of Wallingford. Reading was apparently far smaller. Indeed Reading is one of the puzzles of the early history of the Thames Valley. We have already seen in discussing these strategical points upon the river what advantages it had, and yet it appears only sporadically in ancient history as a military post. The Danes hold it on the first occasion on which we find the site recorded, in the latter half of the ninth century: it has a castle during the anarchy of the twelfth, but it is a castle which soon disappears. It frequently plays a part in the Civil Wars of the seventeenth, but the part it plays is only temporary.

And Reading presents a similar puzzle on the civilian side. It is situated at the junction of two waterways, one of which leads directly from the Thames Valley to the West of England, yet it does not seem to have been of a considerable civil importance until the establishment of its monastery; and even then it is not a town of first-class size or wealth, nor does it take up its present position until quite late in the history of the country.

At the time of the Domesday Survey it actually counts, in the number of recorded enclosures at least, for less than a third of Old Windsor; and we may take it, after making every allowance for possible omissions or for some local custom which withdrew it from the taxing power of the Crown, for little more than a village at that moment.

The size of Oxford at the same period we have already touched upon, but since, like every other inference founded upon Domesday, the matter has become a subject of pretty violent discussion, it will bear, perhaps, a repeated and more detailed examination at this place.

Let us first remember that the latest prejudice from which our historical school has suffered, and one which still clings to its more orthodox section, was to belittle as far as possible the general influence of European civilisation upon England; to exalt, for example, the Celtic missionaries and their work at the expense of St Augustine, to grope for shadowy political origins among the pirates of the North Sea, to trace every possible etymology to a barbaric root, and to make of Roman England and of early Medieval England – that is, of the two Englands which were most fully in touch with the general life of Europe – as small a thing as might be.

In the light of this prejudice, which is the more bitter

because it is closely connected with religion and with the bitter theological passions of our universities, we are always safe in taking the larger as against the smaller modern estimates of wealth, of population and of influence, where either of these civilisations is concerned, and, conversely, we are always safe in taking at the lowest modern estimate the numbers and effect of the barbaric element in our history.

To return to the ground we have already briefly covered, and to establish a comparison with Wallingford, the word 'haga', which we saw to be of such doubtful value in the case of Wallingford, is replaced in Oxford by the word 'mansio'. The taxable units so enumerated are just over 600, but of these much more than half are set down as untaxable or imperfectly taxable under the epithets 'Uasta', 'Uastæ'. What that epithet means we do not know. It may mean anything between 'out of repair', 'excused from taxation because they do not come up to our new standard of the way in which a house in a borough should be kept up, and because we want to give them time to put themselves in order', down to the popular acceptation of the word as meaning 'ruined', or even 'destroyed'.

We know that at the close of the eleventh century, or indeed at any time before the thirteenth, the small man who lived under his own roof would live in a very low house, and that, space for space of ground area, the cubical contents of these poor dwellings would be less than those of modern slums. On the other hand, we know that the population would live much more in the open air, slept much more huddled, and also that a very considerable proportion

– what proportion we cannot say, but probably quite half of a Norman borough – was connected with the huge communal institutions – military, ecclesiastical, and for that matter mercantile, as well – which marked the period. We know that the occupied space stood for very much what is now enclosed by the line of the old walls, and we know that under modern conditions this space, in spite of our great empty public buildings, our sparsely inhabited wealthy houses, and our college gardens, can comfortably hold some 5000 people. We can say, therefore, at a guess, but only at a guess, that the Oxford of the Conquest must have had some 3000 people in it at the very least, and can hardly have had 10,000 at the most. These are wide limits, but anyone who shall pretend to make them narrower is imposing upon his readers with an appearance of positive knowledge which is the charlatanism of the colleges, and pretends to exact knowledge where he possesses nothing but the vague basis of antiquarian conjecture.

It is sufficiently clear (and the reading of any of our most positive modern authorities upon Domesday will make it clearer) that no sort of statistical exactitude can be arrived at for the population of the boroughs in the early Middle Ages. But when we consider that Reading is certainly underestimated, and when we consider the detail in which we are informed of Old Windsor, Wallingford, and Oxford, with the neglect of Abingdon, Lechlade, Cricklade, and Dorchester, one can roughly say that the Thames above London possessed in Staines, Windsor, Cookham, probably Henley, perhaps Bensington, Dorchester, Eynsham, and possibly Buscot, large villages varying from some hundreds

in population to a little over 1000, not defended, not reckoned as towns, and agricultural in character. To these we
may add Chertsey, Ealing, and a few others whose proximity to London makes it difficult for us to judge except in
the vaguest way their true importance.

In another category, possessing a different type of
communal life, already thinking of themselves as towns, we
should have Cricklade, Lechlade, Abingdon, and Kingston
among the smaller, though probably possessing a population not much larger than that of the larger villages; while
of considerable centres there were but three: Reading the
smallest, almost a town, but one upon which we have no
true or sufficient data; Wallingford the largest, with the
population of a flourishing county town in our own days,
and Oxford, a place which, though in worse repair, ran
Wallingford close.

Henley affords an interesting study. At the time of
the Conquest, Bensington was no longer, Henley not yet,
a borough. To trace the growth of Henley is especially
engrossing, because it is one of the very rare examples of a
process which earlier generations of historians, and notably
the popular historians like Freeman and the Rev. Mr Green,
took to be a common feature in the story of this island.
They were wrong, of course, and they have been widely
and deservedly ridiculed for imagining that the greater part
of our English boroughs grew up since the barbarian invasions upon waste places. On the contrary most of our towns
grew up upon Roman and pre-Roman foundations, and are
continuous with the pre-historic past. But Henley forms a
very interesting exception.

It was a hamlet which went with the manor of Bensington, and that point alone is instructive, for it points to the insignificance of the place. When the lords of Bensington went hunting up on Chiltern they found on the far side of the hill, it may be presumed, a little clearing near the river. This was all that Henley was, and it is probable that even the church of the place was not built until quite late in the Christian period; there is at any rate an old tradition that Aldeburgh is the mother of Henley, and it is imagined by those who wrote monographs upon the locality that this tradition points to the church of Aldeburgh as the mother church of what was at first a chapel upon the riverside.

When we first hear of Henley it is already called a town, and the date of this is the first year of King John, 1199.

It must be remembered that the river had been developed and changed in that first century of orderly government under the Normans. Indeed one of the reforms which the aristocracy made much of in their revolt, and which is granted in Magna Charta, is the destruction of the King's weirs upon the Thames. But the weirs cannot have been permanently destroyed; though the public rights over the river were curtailed by Magna Charta, the system of regulation was founded and endured. It is probably this improvement on the great highway which led to the growth of Henley, and when Reading Minster had become the great thing it was late in the twelfth century, Henley must have felt the effect, for it would have afforded the nearest convenient stage down the river from the new and wealthy settlement round the Cluniac Abbey. In the thirteenth century – that is, in the first hundred years after the earliest mention we have of the place – Henley became rapidly more and more important. It seems to have afforded a convenient halting place whenever progress was made up river, especially a royal progress from Windsor. Edward I stayed there constantly, and we possess a record of three dates which are very significant of this kind of journey. In the December of 1277 the King goes up river. On the sixteenth of the month he slept at Windsor, on the seventeenth at Henley, the next day at Abingdon; and in his son's time Henley has grown so much that it counts as one of the three only boroughs in the whole of Oxfordshire: Oxford and Woodstock are the two others.

It was in the thirteenth century also that a bridge was thrown across the river at this point – that is, Henley possessed a bridge long before Wallingford, and at a time when the river could be crossed by road in but very few places. The granting of a number of indulgences, and the promises of masses in the middle of the thirteenth century for this object, give us the date; and, what is perhaps equally interesting, this early bridge was of stone.

It is usual to think of the early bridges over the Thames as wooden bridges. Aft older generation was accustomed to many that still remained. This was true of the later Middle Ages, and of the torpor and neglect in building which followed the Reformation. But it was not true of the thirteenth and fourteenth centuries. The bridge at Henley, like the bridge of Wallingford and the later bridge of Abingdon, was of stone.

It was allowed to fall into decay, and when Leland crossed the river at this point it was upon a wooden bridge, the piers of which stood upon the old foundation. How long that wooden bridge had existed in 1533, when Leland noticed it, we cannot tell, but it remained of wood until 1786, when the present bridge replaced it.

In spite of the early importance of the town, it was not regularly incorporated for a long time, but was governed by a Warden, the first on the list being the date of 1305, within the reign of Edward I. The charter which gave Henley a Mayor and Corporation was granted as late as the reign of Henry VIII and but a few years before Leland's visit. From that moment, however, the town ceased to expand, either in importance or in numbers; the destruction of Reading Abbey and of the Cell of Westminster at Hurley just over the river, very possibly affected its prosperity. At the beginning of the nineteenth century it had a population of less than 3000, and sixty years later it had not added another 1000 to that number.

Maidenhead follows, for centuries, a sort of parallel course to the development of Henley.

Recently, of course, it has very largely increased in population, and in this it is an example in a minor degree of what Reading and Oxford are in a major degree – that is, of the changes which the railway has made in the Thames Valley. But until the effect of the railway began to be felt Maidenhead was the younger and parallel town to Henley.

For example, though we cannot tell exactly when Maidenhead Bridge was built, we may suppose it to have been some few years after Henley Bridge. It already exists and is in need of repair in 1297. Henley Bridge is founded more than a generation earlier than that.

'Maidenhythe', as it was called, has been thought to have been before the building of this bridge a long timber wharf upon the river, but that is only a guess. There must have been some local accumulation of wealth or of traffic or it would not have been chosen as a site for the new bridge which was somewhat to divert the western road.

Originally, so far as we can judge, the main stream of gravel crossed the Thames at Cookham, and again at Henley. Why this double crossing should have been necessary it is useless to conjecture unless one hazards the guess that the quality of the soil in very early times gave so much better going upon the high southern bank of the river that it was worth while carrying the main road along the bank, even at the expense of a double crossing of the stream. If that was the case it is difficult to see how a town of the importance of Marlow could have grown up upon the farther shore; that Marlow was important we know from the fact that it had a Borough representation in Parliament in the first years of that experiment before the close of the thirteenth century.

At any rate, whatever the reason was, whether from some pre-historic conditions having brought the road across the peninsula at this point, or, as is more likely, on account of some curious arrangement of mediæval privilege, it is fairly certain that, in the centuries before the great development of the thirteenth, travel did come across the river in front of Cookham, recross it in front of Henley, and so make over the Chilterns to the great main bridge at Wallingford, which led out to the Vale of the White Horse and the west country.

The importance of Cookham in this section of the road is shown in several ways. First the great market, in Domesday bringing in customary dues to the King of twenty shillings – and what twenty shillings means in Domesday in mere market dues one can appreciate by considering that all the dues from Old Windsor only amounted to ten pounds. Then again it was a royal manor which, unlike most of the others, was never alienated; it was not even alienated during the ruin and breakdown of the monarchy which followed the Dissolution of the monastic orders.

To this day traces remain of the road which joined this market to the second crossing at Henley.

We may presume that the importance of Cookham was maintained for some two centuries after the Conquest, until it was outflanked and the stream of its traffic diverted by the building of the bridge at Maidenhead.

Just as this bridge came later than the Bridge at Henley, so it was inferior to it in structure; it was, as we have seen, of timber, but such as it was, it was the cause of the growth of Maidenhead much more than was the bridge at Henley the cause of the growth of Henley. The first nucleus of municipal government grows up in connection with the Bridge Guild; the Warden and the Bridge Masters remain the head of the embryonic corporation throughout the sixteenth and seventeenth centuries, and even when the town is incorporated (shortly before the close of the seventeenth century), by James II, the maintenance and guardianship of the wooden bridge remained one of the chief occupations of the new corporation.

It was just after the granting of the Charter that the

army of William III marched across this bridge on its way to London, an episode which shows how completely Maidenhead held the monopoly of the Western road. The present stone bridge was not built to replace the old wooden one until the last quarter of the eighteenth century, parallel in this as in everything else to the example of Henley; and this position of inferiority to Henley, and of parallel advance to that town, is further seen in the statistics of population. In 1801, when Henley already boasted nearly 2000 souls, Maidenhead counted almost exactly half that number. The later growth of the place is quite modern.

The antiquity of the crossing of the Thames at Cookham is supported by a certain amount of pre-historic evidence, worth about as much as such evidence ever is, and about as little. Two Neolithic flint knives have been found there, a bronze dagger sheath and spear-head, a bronze sword, and a whole collection or store of other bronze spear-heads. Such as it is, it is a considerable collection for one spot.

Cookham has not only these pre-historic remains; it has also fragments of British pottery found in the relics of pile dwellings near the river, and two Roman vases from the bed of the stream; it has further furnished Anglo-Saxon remains, and, indeed, there are very few points upon the river where so regular a continuity of the historic and the pre-historic is to be discovered as in the neighbourhood of this old ford.

In was in the course of the Middle Ages, and after the Conquest, that new Windsor rose to importance. It is not recognised as a borough before the close of the thirteenth century; it is incorporated in the fifteenth.

Reading certainly increased considerably with the continual stream of wealth that poured from the abbey; it possessed in practice a working corporation before the Dissolution, was famous for its cloth long before, and had become, in the process of years, an important town that rivalled the great monastery which had developed it; indeed it is probable that only the privileges, the conservatism, of the abbey forbade it to be recognised and chartered before the Reformation.

Abingdon also grew (but with less vigour), also had a manufactory of cloth, though of a smaller kind, and was also worthy of incorporation at the end of the Middle Ages.

Staines cannot take its place with these, for in spite of its high strategical value, of its old Roman tradition, of its proximity to London and the rest, Staines was throughout the Middle Ages, and till long after, rather a village than a town. Though a wealthy place it is purely agricultural in the Domesday Survey, and the comparative insignificance of the spot is perhaps explained by the absence of a bridge. That absence is by no means certain. Staines after all was on the great military highway leading from London westward, and it must have been necessary for considerable forces to cross the river here throughout the Dark Ages and the early Middle Ages, as did for instance, at the very close of that period, the barons on their way to Runnymede; and far earlier the army that marched hurriedly from London to intercept the Danes in 1009, when the pagans were coming up the river, and whether by the help of the tide or what not, managed to get ahead of the intercepting force. But if a bridge existed so early as the Conquest, we have no mention of it. The first allusion to a bridge is in the granting of three oaks from Windsor for the repairing of it in 1262. It may have existed long before that date, but it is significant that in the Escheats of Edward III, and as late as the twenty-fourth year of his reign – that is, after the middle of the fourteenth century – it is mentioned that the bridge existed since the reign of Henry III, which would convey the impression that in 1262 the bridge had first needed repairing, being built, perhaps, in the earlier years of the reign and completed, possibly, but a little after the death of King John.

This bridge of Staines was most unfortunate. It broke down again and again. Even an experiment in stone at the end of the last century was a failure, because the foundations did not go deep enough into the bed of the river. An iron absurdity succeeded the stone, and luckily broke down also, until at last, in the thirties of the nineteenth century, the whole thing was rebuilt, 200 yards above the old traditional site.

Staines is of interest in another way, because it marks one of those boundaries between the maritime and the wholly inland part of a river which is in so many of the English valleys associated with some important crossing. The jurisdiction of the port of London over the river extended as high as the little island just opposite the mouth of the Colne. On this island can still be seen the square stone shaft which is at least as old as the thirteenth century (though it stands on more modern steps), and which marks this limit, as it does also the shire mark between Middlesex and Buckingham.

We have, after the Dissolution it is true, and when the financial standing of most of these places had been struck a heavy blow, a valuable estimate for many of them in the inquiry ordered by Pole in 1555. This estimate gives Abingdon less than 1500 of population, Reading less than 3000, Windsor about 1000; and in general one may say that with the sixteenth century, whether the population was diminishing (as certainly contemporary witnesses believed), or whether it had increased beyond the maximum which England had seen before the Black Death, at any rate the relative importance of the various centres of population had not very greatly changed during those long five centuries of customary rule and of firm tradition. The towns and villages which Shakespeare would have passed in a journey up the river, though probably shrunk somewhat from what they had been in, let us say, the days of Edward I or of his grandson, when the Middle Ages were in their full vigour and before the Black Death had ruined our countrysides, were still a string of some such large villages and small walled boroughs as his ancestry had seen for many hundred years, disfigured only and changed by the scaffolded ruins here and there of the great religious foundations. Windsor, Wallingford, Reading, Abingdon, and even Oxford, were towns appearing to him much as Lechlade to-day remains or Abingdon still. As for the riverside villages their agricultural and native population was certainly larger than that which they now possess; and in general the effect produced upon such a journey was of a sort of even distribution of population gradually increasing from the loneliness of the upper river to the growing sites between Windsor and

London, but in no part exaggerated; larger everywhere in proportion to the importance of the stream, or of agricultural or of strategical position, and forming together one united countryside, bound together even in its architecture by the common commerce of the river.

The seventeenth and eighteenth centuries did little to disturb this equilibrium or to destroy this even tradition. The opening up of the waterways and the great improvement of the highroads, and the building of bridges, and the expansion of wealth at the end of the eighteenth century had indeed some considerable effect in increasing the population of England as a whole, but the smaller country towns, in the south at least, and in the Thames Valley, seem to have benefited fairly equally from the general change. The new canals, entering at Oxford and at Reading, gave a certain lead to both those centres, and even the Severn Canal, entering at Lechlade, did a little for that up-river town. The new fashion of the public schools (which had now long been captured by the wealthier classes) also increased the importance of Eton, and towards the close of the period the now rapidly expanding capital had overfed the villages within reach of London with a considerable accession of population. But it is remarkable how evenly spread was even this industrial development.

The twin towns of Abingdon and Reading, for instance, twin monasteries, twin corporations, had for all these centuries preserved their ratio of the up-country town and the larger centre that was the neighbour of London and Windsor. In the beginning of the nineteenth century, in spite of the general increase of population, that ratio was still well preserved: it is about three to one. But the Railway found one and left the other.

The Railway came, and in our own generation that ratio began to change out of all knowledge. It grows from four, five, six, to *seven* to one. After a short halt you have eight, nine and at last – after eighty years – more than *ten* to one. The last census (that of 1901) is still more significant: Abingdon positively declines, and the last ratio is *twelve*.

It is through the Railway, and even then long after its first effect might have been expected, that the Valley of the Thames, later than any other wealthy district in England, loses, as all at last are doomed to lose, its historic tradition, and suffers the social revolution which has made modern England the unique and perilous thing it is among the nations of the world.

INDEX